WONDERS OF VICTORIAN ENGINEERING

An engraver's version of Turner's *Wind, Steam, and Speed.*

WONDERS OF
VICTORIAN
ENGINEERING

AN ILLUSTRATED EXCURSION

BY

ALLEN ANDREWS

JUPITER : LONDON

1978

First published in 1978 by
JUPITER BOOKS (LONDON) LIMITED
167 Hermitage Road, London N4 1LZ
ISBN 0 904041 96 4

Composed in 11-point Monotype Old Style, Series 2,
and printed and bound in Great Britain by
R. J. Acford Limited, Chichester, Sussex.

Only by knowledge of Nature's laws can man subjugate her powers and appropriate her materials for his own purposes. The whole history of arts and inventions is a continued comment on this text; and since the knowledge can be obtained only by observation of Nature, it follows that Science, which is the exact and orderly summing-up of the results of such observation, must powerfully contribute to the well-being and progress of mankind.

LORD MACAULAY

CONTENTS

INTRODUCTION: VICTORIAN WONDERS

THIS BOOK details the progress of nineteenth-century science up to a point exactly a century ago. It is a book of real wonder, as far as the Victorians were concerned, for they had an honest and unsuspecting admiration for science and saw nothing but good in its developments. The heart of the creed was that science was *useful*, and that even the most remotely theoretical discovery would sooner or later be put to material use and benefit in practical life. There was every encouragement for this line of argument at that time. It was science which had shown the way for the introduction of mass production, based on specialisation of labour – and in Victorian times workpeople did not complain about the psychological frustration of doing one monotonous job in a production line, but were in general very glad to get into the factory and out of the cold. Mass production, while still a novelty, had already produced obvious advantages, while any disadvantages had not yet shown themselves. The Victorians recognised that they had in their power the enormous material benefit of cheap production which not only cut the cost of living but raised and broadened the standard of living, so that the comfortably off could aspire to possessing what the affluent had always had, and the poor could undoubtedly live much more comfortably and with many more conveniences. This was a fortunate enough set of circumstances in any respect. But what made the situation infinitely more advantageous was that Britain had a flying start over the rest of the world in applying the results of the Industrial Revolution. In many respects this was indeed an English Revolution, exported by degrees to other lands. Great Britain led the world as an industrial nation, and even a century ago had no fear of being surpassed by the United States: though a little more cautionary foresight might have given them a hint of the scope of the inventions that were about to come out of America. Just as the American Samuel Morse, after residence in England, had gone back to the United States and produced the revolutionary electro-magnetic telegraph, a Scotsman, Alexander Graham Bell, had gone to America, combined a study of electricity with his university post as professor of vocal physiology – and patented the telephone in 1876 in the United States, although in 1877 the echo and fast subsequent exploitation of that patent had not yet reached English ears. There was indeed a complacency about the Victorian attitude to science, but it was entirely understandable. While modern young people glance apprehensively over their shoulder at scientists who they know have already made bombs enough to blow the world to bits and are now dickering with a few more casual uses of plutonium, the most vicious destructive weapon the Victorians could come up with was the dum-dum explosive bullet, which was promptly declared by soldiers to be unsporting against men, but was defended by sportsmen as humane against animals, according to some slightly incomprehensible logic: 'It has been mercifully urged that it is quite sufficient to maim or otherwise render useless an enemy, without blowing him into a shapeless mass or causing increased torture by making the bullet that penetrates the body explode immediately. Explosive bullets or rifle shells have been, and are now, regularly used in shooting elephants, lions, tigers and other larger animals; and the advocates for their use declare that it is more merciful to kill an animal with one blow and a flash, rather than to condemn it to a slow and lingering death by a number of single bullet wounds.' The dum-dum was, in fact, later outlawed for use against men by a Hague Convention on War, which curiously did nothing to prohibit the shrapnel shell which, even fifty years before the Great War, could be fired with accuracy for four miles and, exploding on impact, scattered 500 bullets at a time. An artillery experiment on Dartmoor showed that one field battery using nine-inch shrapnel could kill or disable 20,000 men in one hour.

But we over-estimate today the social importance of war in the nineteenth century. There was always a war going on, against some quaint Fuzzy-wuzzy or other, but by the same token there were always grouse being shot in Yorkshire in August and partridges in Sussex in November. It was all a part of Nature's blood-letting, and scarcely got into the newspapers unless the enemy was someone really rather nice, like the Russians – for it is another mark of the time that the Russians, whom we were fighting in the Crimea in 1854, were considered pretty charming people, especially in the officer class, while our own Allies, the Turks and the French, were from the rank of general downwards considered unspeakable debauchees only differing from each other in that the Turks were homosexual and the French heterosexual, and many a silk-moustached young Guards officer could not make up his mind which was worse.

The Victorians wondered far more at the marvels of science applied to the peaceful pursuit of prosperity. Heavy manufacturing industries, communications like the railways, canals, alpine tunnels – these were the marvels that excited them most. It will be seen from passages in the following pages that a feasible scheme for the construction of a Channel Tunnel was finalised in 1868 and might well have become a practical project if the Emperor Napoleon III had not been beaten in war by the Prussians and subsequently deposed as a result of the Paris Commune: the prospect of both Prussians and Communards taking excursion trains to Dover was too serious to contemplate.

Lord Macaulay, who was one year old when the nineteenth century began, summed up the attitude of his contemporaries to Science with more even than his usual grandiloquence but accurately enough in his scope: 'It has lengthened human life; it has mitigated pain; it has extinguished diseases; it has increased the fertility of the soil; it has given new securities to the mariner; it has furnished new arms to the warrior; it has spanned great rivers and estuaries with bridges of form unknown to our fathers; it has guided the thunderbolt innocuously from heaven to earth; it has lighted up the night with the splendour of the day; it has extended the range of the human vision; it has multiplied the power of the human muscles; it has accelerated motion; it has annihilated distance; it has facilitated intercourse, correspondence, all friendly offices, all despatch of business; it has enabled man to descend to the depths of the sea, to soar into the air, to penetrate securely into the noxious recesses of the earth, to traverse the land in cars which whirl along without horses, to cross the ocean in ships which run ten knots an hour against the wind. These are but part of its fruits, and of its first-fruits; for it is a philosophy which never rests, which has never attained, which is never perfect. Its law is progress. A point which yesterday was invisible is its goal today, and will be its starting-point tomorrow.'

WONDERS OF VICTORIAN ENGINEERING

The apparatus for making Bessemer Steel.

ONE
THE HEART OF THE MATTER: IRON

THE VICTORIANS considered iron and coal the kings of the earth, and the selective and skilful use of the two in the Bessemer process converting crude pig iron into steel was one of the basic utilitarian marvels of the age. But it should be remembered that the Bessemer process, though it was still in use a century later, was modified by the refining patent of Thomas Gilchrist in 1878 and this is not covered in the contemporary descriptions. The men of the time saw iron as the most common of the metals, the ore not only being found in abundance, but the metal being to some proportion a constituent of every natural mineral found – as well as being present in flesh and vegetable matter. Though iron as found on earth was never pure and had always to be smelted from the ore, it was considered a remarkable fact that meteorites which fell from space usually consisted of little else but pure iron with a trace of nickel. The maximum weight of a fallen meteorite then known was one of fourteen tons which fell in South America. Owing to the irregularity – indeed, the complete cessation – of further deliveries, no manufacturer set up an iron foundry on the spot where it was discovered: but meteorites of lesser bulk used to fall in India with at least enough frequency for the Indians to recognise them and forge acceptable swords from them.

The chief source of the iron produced in Great Britain was the clay ironstone found in South Wales and Staffordshire. This contained an impure carbonate of iron mixed with clay, lime, manganese oxide and impurities. Though poor in its percentage of iron content its advantage was that the ore was mined in areas where other strata in the earth produced necessary lime and coal. In olden days iron was produced simply by heating the ore alongside charcoal and raising the temperature of the fire with bellows. But clay ironstone had to be smelted into cast iron, that is, layers of ore and layers of coal were heaped in a chamber and burnt. The constituents were in fact roasted in the oven for several months and the resulting mass was put into a blast furnace. The furnace was so called because there was a literal blast of air, constantly propelled at a pressure of three pounds a square inch. The furnaces were never extinguished until they needed repair – possibly at intervals of ten years. They were charged with layers of coal and the roasted ore, with the addition of limestone fragments, introduced in order to make the clay and other impurities melt and run more easily. These unwanted constituents continually flowed out from the furnace as slag.

The air blasted into the furnace quickly lost its oxygen and was converted to carbon monoxide, a combustible gas which took both carbon and oxygen from the ore and discharged the material in the slag. The resulting iron, however, still contained from two to five per cent of carbon when it was regularly drawn off to solidify in the bars known as pig iron. This cast iron also contained silicon, manganese and other metals. On average among the various types, cast iron was ninety per cent pure iron. The different cast irons produced had varying qualities of malleability and brittleness. It could not be wrought with the hammer, rolled into plates, or welded on an anvil. For most practical purposes it had therefore to be converted into wrought iron by refining or puddling, in order to remove the carbon and other impurities. It was re-heated on the hearth of a furnace and exposed to air, which oxidised the unwanted elements. The iron itself fused into a spongy mass and was removed by the puddler in balls weighing some seventy pounds to which the melted impurities still clung as slag. The blooms were taken over by the shingler, who hammered them or compresssed them between rollers while still hot, forcing the iron into a compact mass and squeezing out the slag. Finally it was rolled into bars, cut into lengths, and re-heated and re-rolled to impart greater strength. It came from the rolling mill as wrought iron, still containing from one-fifth to one-half of one per cent of carbon.

Steel contained rather more carbon, up to about one-and-a-half per cent, and it was manufactured to possess the best qualities of both. It was far stronger than wrought iron, the best one-inch steel bar at that time reaching a breaking strain of 120 tons – that is, it would break only under a load of 120 tons. It could be made soft or hard, tough or elastic. It was made either by stopping the refining process while sufficient carbon still remained in the iron, or by re-combining wrought iron with carbon, heating the wrought iron in a closed oven for a week with powdered charcoal.

The method of the partial decarbonisation of cast iron was abandoned after the Bessemer process was introduced. Henry Bessemer, later Sir Henry, discovered that carbon and silicon could be effectively removed from molten pig iron by forcing currents of cold air through the mass of fused metal, the force of the air supplanting the action of the puddler with his stirring rod. In 1855 Bessemer took out his first patent for 'forcing currents of air, or of steam, or of air and steam, into and among the particles of molten crude iron, or of re-melted pig, or refined iron, until the metal so treated is thereby rendered malleable, and has acquired other properties common to cast steel, and still retaining the fluid state of such metal, and pouring or running the same into suitable moulds.' Fairly soon he found that steam had an injurious effect, and that by using air alone he could raise the temperature of the metal from a red to a white heat. He used a cylindrical converter in the bottom of which were many clay nozzles, called *tuyères*, through which air was blasted which kept the liquid metal in a constant stir.

The process was unsuccessful at first because, although the carbon and silicon were removed, quantities of phosphorus and sulphur remained, and a proportion as low as seven parts of phosphorus in ten thousand meant that the product had to be rejected. The situation was saved by Mushet's innovation of adding a determined proportion of manganese to the metal to be fired. Some five to ten per cent of the contents of the converter were made up from spiegeleisen (German for mirror-iron), a white, hard cast-iron which, when broken, showed mirror-like crystals indicating a large proportion of manganese in the original ore. This greatly improved the quality of the steel.

The Bessemer converter was adapted into an egg-shaped receptacle some 3½ feet at its maximum diameter, made of wrought iron in two roughly similar parts, like an egg-cup upside down on another egg-cup, and these halves could be bolted together. At the top of the lower egg-cup were trunnions like cannon-mountings on which the converter could swing. The vessel was lined with a thick coating of ground fire-bricks and sandstone incapable of melting. One of the trunnions was

A blast furnace.

hollow and enclosed a pipe which admitted the air blast to a chamber in the bottom of the vessel from which the air was blown through fifty half-inch-diameter holes, set, however, not in the bottom but in the sides at about one-third of the height of the entire converter, nearing the top of the lower 'egg-cup'. The other trunnion extended to a toothed wheel engaging a rack which moved up and down by hydraulic power, turning the wheel. The iron for the operation was melted in a furnace which discharged above the level of the converter. When the furnace was tapped the molten iron was passed into the top of the converter, after it had been inclined, by way of a trough lined with sand. The converter was therefore swung until it was almost horizontal. The metal was allowed to pour in until its surface was nearly at the top of the lowest holes through which the air entered. Usually the capacity of the converter was about five tons of molten iron treated at one time, but it was normal practice to have a circle of converters all of which could be fed through the trough from the melting-furnace. While the converter was still horizontal the air blast was turned on at a pressure of fifteen pounds per square inch. Then the hydraulically-operated column and wheel were activated and the converter slowly swung into its upright position. The pressure of the air blast prevented any of the molten iron from entering the blow-holes. Once upright, the blast of cold air was continued for between twelve and twenty minutes until all the silicon and carbon had been consumed. Then the converter was swung back to its horizontal position and a predetermined weight of melted cast iron of the required composition, which of course contained the manganese ingredient, was run in. The blowing was resumed, the vessel was swung upright, and the blast was continued for some five minutes more while the turbulence inside thoroughly mixed the constituents. Then the converter was swung down again and the blast was shut off. The contents of the converter were run off into a vessel of wrought iron, lined with sand and fitted with an iron plug coated with sand and fitting into a socket. The plug was raised, and the molten steel was allowed to flow out into moulds, the stream being about an inch in diameter. The steel had therefore been made, not by stopping decarbonisation, but by adding the carbon and manganese and other chosen ingredients – sometimes small proportions of silver, rhodium and chromium were added for special purposes – so that the required composition of steel was obtained.

[19]

The records of the Institute of Civil Engineers contain a graphic description of the physical impact of the process:

The air, introduced in powerful jets, springs upward through the fluid mass. Expanding in volume, the air divides itself into globules, or bursts violently upwards, carrying with it some hundredweights of fluid metal, which again falls into the boiling mass below. Every part of the apparatus trembles under the violent agitation thus produced. A roaring flame rushes from the mouth of the vessel, and as the process advances it changes its violet colour to orange, and finally to a voluminous pure white flame. The sparks, which at first were large like those of ordinary foundry iron, change to small hissing points, and these gradually give way to small floating specks of bluish light as the state of malleable iron is approached. There is no eruption of cinder, although it is formed during the process; the improved shape of the converter causes it to be retained, and it not only acts beneficially on the metal, but it helps to confine the heat, which during the process has risen from the comparatively low temperature of melted pig iron to one vastly greater than the highest known welding heat, by which malleable iron only becomes sufficiently soft to be shaped by the blows of the hammer. But here it becomes perfectly fluid, and even rises so much above the melting point as to admit of its being poured from the converter into a foundry ladle, and from thence transferred to several successive moulds.

A century ago the process was still not perfect, but the method had already allowed new developments in the applications of steel. Five tons of malleable metal had been produced from pig iron in one of many converters working simultaneously but in stepped progression, all in the period of half an hour, and this mass of metal was in a state of perfect fusion. Steel, formerly so expensive that it was used only for knives and springs, was now produced in quantities (some 400,000 tons a year in 1875) which allowed it to be used for the construction of bridges, railways and buildings where its strength, hardness, elasticity and durability were required. When Bessemer stepped up the capacity of his converters to an occasional maximum of ten tons, steel castings of that weight were available whereas formerly a hundredweight steel casting would have been an achievement. With this revolutionary expansion of the practical application of steel, the modern machine-tool industry was born. Henceforth men could use steel to make massive tools with which other machines could be manufactured – machines which depended on utter precision in their own character to impose dependable precision on what they made. This is the absolute requirement of all mass-manufacture.

[20]

TWO
THE BEST USE OF STEAM

THE NINETEENTH CENTURY was presented with the steam engine in its cradle, for Watt's development of the Newcomen stationary steam engine was already in common use. The principle was steadily refined during Victoria's reign, the most notable single advance being Giffard's steam injector by which the water constantly evaporating in the boiler of a steam engine was replenished by the application of a jet of steam. In a great forward dart into the scientific future Henri Giffard, the inventor of this device, put it up into the air, and in 1852 installed his steam engine into an airship, achieved a speed of five miles an hour with a highly inefficient propeller, and became the first man in the world to drive a navigable and dirigible (steerable) airship. But apart from this notable exception steam power was to be mainly earthbound, with a future directed towards driving wheels to motivate belts that turned stationary machines, or wheels that used friction against a (comparatively) horizontal surface to achieve longitudinal motion. The first locomotive of any consequence was running in 1804. The early models were mechanically inefficient, and were used only to draw industrial loads by means of toothed driving wheels which engaged in racks laid on the ground as rails. In 1813 the discovery was made that in favourable conditions the rack-and-tooth method was unnecessary, and, given sufficient weight, the bite of a smooth wheel on a smooth rail was enough to achieve traction. George Stephenson devised the blast pipe, and later the tubular boiler, and he incorporated these innovations in his famous *Rocket* which on 6 October 1829 won the competition instigated by the directors of the Liverpool and Manchester Railway. The *Rocket* weighed $4\frac{1}{2}$ tons and at its successful demonstration drew a load of tenders and carriages weighing 12¾ tons at an average speed of 14 miles an hour and a maximum speed of 29 m.p.h. Stephenson's success initiated the Railway Age, and by the date of Victoria's accession there were 1500 miles of railway in the country: by 1870 there were 13,600 miles. At that time the weight of a locomotive could be 50 tons, its load could be up to 500 tons, and its laden speed could reach 60 miles an hour.

In construction the locomotive of a century ago, though it has a quaint image now, was a highly-regarded and comparatively efficient piece of machinery. The boiler space was cylindrical, lagged with thick layers of felt and long laths of wood to contain them, and covered with thin sheet iron as the external protection. The fire-box was inset into one end of the boiler, so that it was surrounded on all sides by water except where the furnace door opened on to the footplate. Below the fire-box was the grate where cinders could drop for constant removal. At the front end of the locomotive was the chimney, which was still outstandingly tall. Beneath it was the smoke-box and this was connected to the fire-box by some 300 brass pipes, open at both ends and firmly fixed into the end plates of the boiler. These tubes, up to two inches in diameter, presented a large heating surface to the water, which covered them and the top of the fire-box. The water was carried in a tender and the boiler was replenished by the action of a Giffard's injector or a more old-fashioned pump. The steam left the boiler by a pipe leading into the steam dome, usually at this time at the driver's end of the locomotive. The steam then entered another pipe leading forwards along the top of the boiler but above the water level to avoid any cooling action. The steam passed through the regulator, a throttle which governed the quantity allowed through, and the pipe divided at the smoke-box to go down to the cylinders, one on each side of the locomotive at the front end. The steam was admitted into the cylinders by slide-valves, and after working the pistons alternately escaped up through the blast pipe leading into the chimney, increasing the draught of the fire by drawing the fire-box flame through the tubes in proportion to the regulated rush of steam. Each cylinder had a piston, connecting rod, and crank, with the cranks working so that when the one on the port side was at dead point the one on the starboard side was taking the full power of the piston. Up to three pairs of wheels were coupled for drive: at that time bogeys were not in use. A steam pressure of 120 pounds on each square inch of the boiler was not unusual. Boilers blew up with disastrous consequences

A section of an early steam locomotive.

through the sudden generation of a large quantity of steam – either through so low a level of water in the boiler that too much cold water was suddenly introduced and converted into steam, or through excessive deposits of scale within the boiler caused by hard water.

The application of steam power as the fundamental prime mover for all transport had been foreseen before the nineteenth century, when Erasmus Darwin, the scientist grandfather of Charles Darwin and Francis Galton, prophesied:

> Soon shall thy arm, unconquer'd steam! afar
> Drag the slow barge, or drive the rapid car;
> Or on wide-waving wings expanded bear
> The flying chariot through the field of air.

The unexpected application of steam to 'the flying chariot through the field of air' has already been noted. As for 'driving the rapid car', the first steam automobile had emerged three years before the first practical railroad locomotive, and had respectable antecedents before that. The unlikely scene of both locomotive and automobile research at the end of the eighteenth century was in the county of Cornwall, where the application of the steam engine to mining was being enthusiastically followed. William Murdock, an assistant of James Watt, built a model steam carriage in 1784, a three-wheeler which confidently applied the principle of the conversion of lateral motion to circular rotation by a crank – one of the most revolutionary 'simple ideas' that any man ever thought of in his bath. Murdock got his puffing miniature on the road one night at Redruth, where it provoked a gratifying increase in Cornish piety, already accelerated by the Wesleyan revival. For the car ran away at an unanticipated speed, and scared the wits out of the local parson, who was convinced it was a manifestation of the Devil. Murdock improved his design, but could not exploit it. For James Watt – some say in jealousy – assigned to his assistant a suffocating increase in work on the development of the stationary engine.

Another Cornish mining engineer, Richard Trevithick, made his own model steam carriage, and celebrated the opening of the nineteenth century in 1801 by developing it that year to full-size proportions as a 60-pound boiler-pressure steamer. With his cousin Andrew Vivian he made a trial run on Christmas Eve. It took eight people up Camborne Beacon – a hill up the road from Redruth, and still an occasional terror for motorists on Christmas Eve – with the burly Trevithick (he was a notable wrestler and weight-lifter) at the controls, going faster than walking pace. The steamers always were supreme on hills. Trevithick patented and improved his steam car, which had a horizontal boiler and engine transmitting through a crankshaft geared to the main road wheels by cogged spur wheels. Later one of his carriages was briefly worked in London on a Holborn-to-Paddington coach service. If he had had recognisable commercial success he would have introduced the change-speed gear, for he had already proposed that 'the power of the engine with regard to its convenient application to the carriage may be varied by changing the relative velocity of rotation of the road wheels, compared to that of the crank axis, by shifting the gears or toothed wheels for others of different size properly adapted to each other.' But inventors must live on quick returns, and Trevithick side-tracked to railway locomotives and mining engines, lost his money in South America, and died penniless.

He survived to see the full flowering of road steamers. The British had responded to the new sport – for it was always sport, even when the carriages were camouflaged as commercial vehicles – with delighted acclaim. Sir Goldsworthy Gurney, another Cornishman, gave up his career as a doctor in 1823 and transferred to locomotion, inventing among other things the high-pressure steam jet. Gurney built steam carriages and ran them down the old faithful Bath Road, now given a gratifying new surface by Macadam. One machine he drove was a six-wheeler, steered by two front wheels pivoting with a central tiller, and aided on hills by mechanical legs which he had patented – nothing short of a series of Isle of Man symbols, three legs radiating from the centre of a circle, which revolved on a low-slung axis and dug their heels into the road when additional power was required for the gradients. Gurney was in fact running express bus services in England before Victoria came to the throne. There were occasional little local difficulties. Held up in a crowd at Melksham Fair, the coach and passengers were attacked by Luddite farm labourers as a dangerous example of modern machinery and its devilish operators. Gurney was badly hurt and his fireman, having been knocked cold, suffered the indignity of having to be taken for surgical treatment to Bath in a horse-drawn post-chaise. Gurney, when not hampered by sit-down demonstrations, was clocking some respectable speeds. On a 'continuous' journey from London to Bath and back he ran the last eighty-four miles from Melksham to Cranford in ten hours. One must call the trips 'continuous' and not non-stop, because there were very frequent and necessary stoppages for drawing fresh water from the ponds and streams carefully marked on the route-map. But Gurney could keep up a cruising speed of 12 miles an hour and achieved a top speed of some 25 miles an hour – some sixteen per cent down on the performance of the contemporary *Rocket* and of course managing a far smaller pay-load, but without the laying down of any railroad tracks at all. Gurney was exploiting to the full the potential for convenience and spontaneity of mechanical road transport.

Walter Hancock, building machines which were either five-wheelers steered by a single front wheel or straight four-wheelers, ran a London bus service by steam carriage in 1834, incorporating in his machine for the first time a clutch to throw the engine out of gear, so that the feed pump and furnace fan could still operate when the car was stationary. By introducing this sort of refinement he sometimes suffered from a lack of skill on the part of his engineers. One would-be speedster running Hancock's Enterprise coach between Paddington and the City over-exposed his enterprise by trying to get spectacular starts on full power after his halts at every bus-stop. He fastened the safety-valve tight with copper wire, developed a forced draught before moving off, and never did move off, but only up, for he blew himself to pieces before he had time to collect the fares. He was certainly fast off the grid. But even for more orthodox operators speeds began to mount. A pioneer called Ogle touched 35 miles an hour on a trip from London to Southampton, and soared over a one-in-six hill at 16½ miles an hour with a three-ton pay-load. A Select Committee of the House of Commons gave a most friendly welcome to the new form of transport. It reported:

The substitution of inanimate for animal power, in draught on common roads, is one of the most important improvements in the means of internal communications ever introduced. Its general adoption will take place more or less rapidly, in proportion as the attention of specific men shall be drawn by public encouragement to further improvements. One formidable obstacle will arise from the prejudices which always beset a new invention, especially one which will at first appear detrimental to the interests of so many indi-viduals. Tolls to the amount which would utterly prohibit the introduction of steam carriages have been imposed on some roads; on others, the trustees have adopted modes of apportioning the charge, which would be found, if not

[26]

absolutely prohibitory, at least to place such carriages in a very unfair position as compared with ordinary coaches.

Parliament had spotlighted the powerful opposition to the steamers. And the toll-farmers won. On the Ashburton-to-Totnes road in Devon the rate for Gurney's steam carriage was set at £2 against only three shillings charged for a fully loaded stage coach. It was a twelvefold differential of £2. 8s. against four shillings between Liverpool and Prescot. 'The trustees of the Liverpool and Prescot Road,' mourned the Select Committee, 'have already obtained the sanction of the legislators to charge the monstrous toll of 1s. 6d. per "horse-power", as if it were a national object to prevent the possibility of such machines being used.' That was an exact definition of the object. The recommendations of the Select Committee to lower tolls were rejected. Steam cars were taxed off the roads by 1840, and Parliament screwed the rack tighter in 1865 with its notorious Locomotive Act requiring a man to walk one hundred yards ahead of any self-propelled vehicle, carrying a red flag by day and a red lamp at night. The red flag went in 1878, but the punitive foot-pace speed limit remained. Henceforth only rich enthusiasts had steam cars built for them, and they ran them surreptitiously like smugglers at dead of night, as the pioneer William Murdock had done almost a century before. Automobile locomotion was dead in Britain until 1896.

The only people to beat the ban were the descendants of the old toll trustees, the busy newly-created city fathers with one hand in local administration and the other in the till of new transport enterprises. Exactly a century ago an observer commented:

The application of steam power to the propulsion of vehicles along common roads has fallen into neglect, but the common road locomotive is at present receiving some attention. In the tramways which are now laid along the main roads in most large cities we see one-half of the problem solved. It is not so much mechanical difficulties which stand in the way of this economical system of locomotion, as the prejudices and interests which have always to be overcome before the world can profit by new inventions. The engines can be made noiseless, emitting no visible steam or smoke, and they are under more perfect control than horses. But vestries and parochial authorities offer such objections as that horses would be frightened in the streets if the engine made a noise; and if it did not, people would be liable to be run over and the horses would be as much startled as in the other case. But horses would soon become accustomed to the sight of a carriage moving without equine aid, however startling the matter might appear to them at first; and the objection urged against the noiseless engines might be alleged against wooden pavements, india-rubber tires, and many other improvements. It is highly probable that in the course of a few years the general adoption of steam-propelled vehicles will displace horses, at least upon tramways. The slowness with which inventions of undeniable utility and of proved advantage come into general use may be illustrated by the fact of the city of Manchester, a great centre of the engineering industry, not having as yet a single tramway, while in all the populous cities of the United States, and in almost every European capital, tramways have been in successful operation for years.

People were guessing about the future, then as now, for no one knew which in particular of any batch of new inventions they should whole-heartedly back – just as after the Second World War, in which record-ing by wire had been developed and exploited both for military com-munications and to some degree for radio despatches from the Front, commercial speculators strongly backed wire-recorders both for business communication and for home entertainment: but magnetic tape quickly supplanted wire-recording because of its greater convenience. A century ago the prophets forecast that before very long it would be quite com-mon to have domestic tasks like grinding coffee, mincing meat and cleaning knives done by steam power. By that time a miniature steam engine had been put on the market which really was a pocket machine, small enough to be carried in a Victorian pocket, and it was sold to be attached to domestic sewing machines which, it was claimed, could be operated at double the old speed at a cost of one halfpenny an hour. The engine consisted of an oscillating cylinder which was connected with its boiler by a flexible india-rubber tube. There had to be another rather longer tube attached to run from the worktable to the window-sill where it had to be jammed under the sash window to allow the waste steam to escape into the open air, rather than convert Madame's drawing room into a Turkish bath. The boiler, tastefully ornamented to indicate that it was not industrial, was heated by gas or paraffin. The speed was regulated by a lever which was connected to a foot-throttle very similar to that in the modern motor car, so that full speed was attained with the foot flat down, and the machine idled when the foot was off the throttle. Many applications of this portable steam engine were envis-aged, but the ladies of Great Britain evinced some distaste for having an industrial power plant, however petite and fancifully decorated, in their rooms. It was so bad for the hair. A larger series of portable steam engines did come into use. They had started with the agricultural steam engine, a monster shaped very like a railway locomotive, which was drawn by horses from point to point on a farm. They had one cylinder placed horizontally above the boiler, and the piston-rod, working in guides as in railway engines which were by then old-fashioned, was attached by a connecting rod to the back of a shaft which carried a fly-wheel, eccentrics and pulleys for belts to conduct the power to the machines to be used. Thomas Hardy has a very interesting account of a harvest reaping being done by these machines in *Jude the Obscure*. In the domestic field the ill-fated portable steam engine for sewing and mincing was overtaken by the introduction of the neater, cleaner, electric motor. Only with the vacuum cleaner did steam very temporarily take over in the chores of the Victorian housewife.

The first practical railway locomotive had run in Great Britain in 1801. The first successful steamboat was the *Charlotte Dundas*, which was towing two seventy-ton barges on the Forth and Clyde Canal in 1802, and making such a speed that the use of the ship was forthwith prohibited on the spot on the excuse that it would wash away the banks of the canal. Between Luddites and the vested interests, progress never had much of a chance: the first installation of a mechanical pump intended to propel a boat, nearly a century previously on the Rhine, had resulted in the destruction of the craft by local boatmen and almost fatal injuries to the inventor. The American Robert Fulton, who had been concerned with the development of steamships for over twenty years before the *Charlotte Dundas* but had never achieved original success, saw this craft in action through the goodwill of its master, master-designer and master-builder, an expert mechanic named William Symington who has never secured an adequate place in the history books. He went home and, on the basis of what he had seen, built the steamer *Clermont* and inaugurated a passenger service from New York to Albany, accomplishing the 150-mile journey on the Hudson river in 32 hours upsteam and 30 hours downstream. The service was so successful that he built two more ships. In the meantime the *Comet* (1804) and two other vessels had started a service on the Clyde. The first steamship operating on the Thames was the *Marjory*, which was run as a steam-packet for hire. In 1825 the first steamship reached India. The first steamship to cross the Atlantic was a 438-ton wooden paddle-steamer

[29]

built at Dover for the Dutch Government, which set out from Rotterdam in April 1827 and reached the other side after a month. Originally a warship named the *Curaçao*, she was re-designated as a mail ship, the *Calpe*, and employed on the West Indies service. Samuel Cunard built a much more efficient vessel, the *Royal William*, which crossed from Halifax to London in 17 days in 1833. On 8 April 1838 the Great Western Railway's magnificent new ship the *Great Western* sailed from Bristol for New York and, arriving in 15 days, inaugurated a regular transatlantic service. A new era was launched when Brunel, who had designed the *Great Western*, built the *Great Britain*, also for the transatlantic run. She was of immense size, compared with her predecessors, being 320 feet long, made of iron, and driven by a screw propeller. This one screw, compared with the two paddles of the others, drove the large ship across in fourteen days.

The screw had been developed by John Ericsson, a Swede who came to England in 1826 at the age of 23 and built railway locomotives and naval steam engines. He invented the propeller in 1836, went to America soon afterwards, and in 1862 built the first American armoured turret ship, the *Monitor*. Iron construction was introduced at the same time as the screw, and the first great iron steamship, the *Rainbow*, operated between London, Ramsgate and Antwerp from 1838. It required considerable effort to overcome the prejudice against iron ships. Iron is clearly heavier than wood, but in order to attain the required strength much less iron is necessary. And an iron ship, being lighter than a wooden vessel, has more buoyancy. Wood needs to be nearly as heavy as its cargo, while an iron craft can carry twice its own weight.

In 1858 the engineer Isambard Kingdom Brunel, who besides building many canals and bridges and the whole of the original Great Western Railway had also designed the *Great Western* and the *Great Britain*, launched his most unlucky ship, the *Great Eastern*, which in spite of failing in its original purpose was still regarded a century ago as a notable Victorian wonder. The ship was, in fact, fifty years ahead of its time. She was twice as long as the ships of the period: 692 feet – a length which was not exceeded by any ship until 1899. She had accommodation for 4000 passengers. She was of double-skinned cellular construction, having an inner and an outer hull of three-quarter-inch iron plates with a ribbed space of almost three feet in between. With an enormous displacement of 24,000 tons, she was driven by two paddle

The *Great Eastern* during construction.

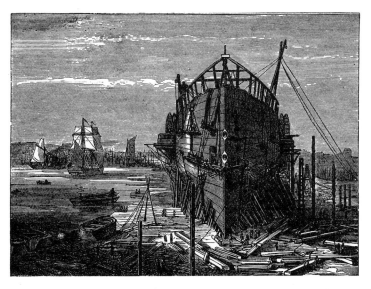

The *Great Eastern* prior to launching.

wheels of 58 feet diameter and a four-bladed screw propeller of 24 feet diameter driven by an engine of four cylinders requiring six boilers and 72 furnaces. Besides five funnels she had six masts which carried 6500 square yards of sail. She burnt twelve tons of coal an hour but carried forty days' supply, on an optimistic calculation that she could steam right round the world without refuelling. Brunel saw her set out on her first voyage on 7 September 1859, and he died eight days later, which was perhaps the most merciful action that Providence could take on his behalf. Her speed was found to be only fifteen knots. She was damaged by a gale at the outset in Holyhead harbour. In a further gale in mid-Atlantic her rudder and paddles were damaged to such an extent that she rolled about helplessly for several days. When she was approaching New York she ran on a rock which stripped the outer plates off the bottom for a length of eighty feet – though her cellular construction proved itself admirably and she suffered no permanent harm. After being repaired the *Great Eastern* steamed home, but confidence in her was shaken, the expected contract to employ her for passenger and mail transport on the long sea route to India did not materialise, and – both Brunels, father and son, having been extremely unpractical financiers – the owning companies were involved in such heavy liabilities that they sold the vessel, which had cost half a million pounds, for a third of her scrap value at £25,000.

The *Great Eastern* fought back, however, and won permanent prestige. She was re-fitted as a cable ship and carried out the task – which no other vessel then built could have accomplished – of laying the whole length of the Atlantic Telegraph cable in 1865. She took on board 2600 miles of cable weighing 5000 tons, and the laying operation was completed successfully. She was then exclusively employed on cable-laying and remained, even until the end of the period presently under review, the largest ship in the world, being from six to seven times the size of any rival – warship or passenger packet – with three times the steam power of the then largest transatlantic liner. She was in fact broken up in 1889.

Another Victorian wonder was described when it was unveiled in 1874 as the most novel and most ingenious invention yet recorded in connection with steam navigation. Unhappily this was not fifty years before its time, but a hundred. Yet the inventor pressed on and had his expensive product built. Fortunately this inventor could afford to lose the money, for he was Henry Bessemer who had made a million pounds out

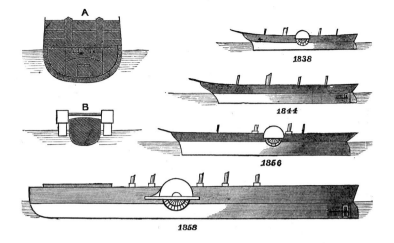

Relative sizes of steamships: 1838 – *Great Western*; 1844 – *Great Britain*; 1856 – *Persia*; 1858 – *Great Eastern*.

Sections (both on same scale): A – the *Great Eastern* amidships; B – the *Great Western* amidships.

of his patent for Bessemer steel converters. He had a number of additional minor inventions to his credit, including the production of gold paint and a moveable die for embossed stamps. Now he set to to build a super-ship. There was an admirable versatility about those Victorian inventors in the palmy days when people were not put off by the jealousy of professional bodies which over-emphasise specialisation. Bessemer determined to design a ship that would abolish sea-sickness. That was an admirable objective, for since in those days people could only leave this island realm by sea they were persistently subjected to an importunate tax on their high spirits and even their health immediately they left. Although the working class were not then seafaring travellers except when they were being sent out as soldiers in one of the frequent colonial wars, there was a very considerable commercial and middle-class traffic. Great Britain was still the salesman to the world, which demanded frequent business trips to Europe as well as to the far-flung empire, and in addition there was leisure enough at that time for a quite extraordinary level of middle-class tourism and holiday-making. The north coast of France was then the Margate of the bourgeoisie, married couples went constantly to Paris for culture and bachelors for sport, Cook's Tours were already shepherding droves of spinsters on extremely athletic walks through Switzerland, and the English tourist occupation of the Rhine was far more concentrated than at any time in the next century. The cross-Channel packets were therefore in constant use by the middle classes, and sea-sickness their frequent conversational topic– as the number of jokes on the subject in any old copy of *Punch* will corroborate. When, therefore, Bessemer announced that he was to build a Channel steamer – and a big one, too – especially designed to combat the old enemy, he had a large and influential public in his pocket from the start.

The saloon of the *Bessemer* was suspended on pivots. The inventor intended that it should be kept in a permanently level position by hydraulic rams which a sailor was to operate through levers as he attempted to counter the continual rolling and pitching of the ship. This was an ambitious proposition, since the reactions of one man had to be relied on to adjust the level of a swinging superstructure that was being subjected to different stresses every second. But Bessemer, before his design was complete, hit on the attractive idea of installing a large gyroscope, setting a very heavy disc spinning rapidly in the horizontal

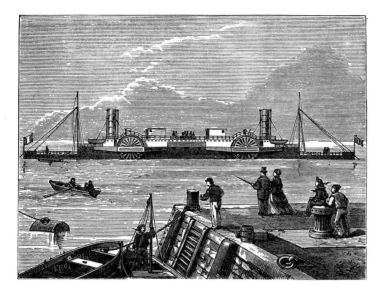

Bessemer steamer.

plane and using the massive force of this highly stable system to move the valves of his hydraulic apparatus and keep his swinging saloon as persistently horizontal as the gyroscope itself. He constructed a very large and very low ship, 350 feet long but with only four feet of free-board in the fore and aft sections, which were each 48 feet long and each fitted with a rudder. The identical fore and aft parts were rounded into a cigar shape and fitted with capstans for use during docking, but it was anticipated that anywhere out of harbour the sea would be breaking over them and it was not anticipated that they would be occupied even by the crew. The middle section had a further eight-feet-high breast-work erected all along its 254-feet length, and this breastwork supported a deck with smoking-rooms, refreshment bars and cabins for families. The swinging saloon took up 90 feet of the space amidships, and was intended for first-class passengers only, but after allowance had been made for external stairways the interior of the saloon was seventy feet long and half as wide. The stairways led to an open deck for the enjoy-ment of the sea breeze but, with pardonable caution in case the sea air should prove too much – or the levelling action of the gyroscope fail to work – retiring-rooms were provided 'where passengers could withdraw from the public gaze'. Between the main saloon and the top deck was a spacious ladies' cabin and two other cabins available for others who demanded privacy. Similar accommodation was also provided for second-class passengers but in their case there was no hope of a swinging saloon, and the space allocated to them was smaller.

The *Bessemer* was fitted with four paddles, two in tandem on each side, though the stern paddles moved faster than the 32 revolutions per minute of the forward paddles since they were taking the wash of the leading paddles. The engines were expected to develop 5000 horse power and to give the ship a speed of twenty miles an hour. There were many innovations which then were modern: all orders from the bridge were conveyed to the engineers by telegraph, and the levers were so concen-trated that one man could work all the engines by himself if required. There was efficient ventilation, an adequate kitchen, a derrick to handle the luggage and a compartmentalised hold to avoid the tossing about of the luggage on the voyage, which was then a considerable nuisance to cross-Channel travellers. Four life-boats and two patented large life-rafts were also carried. Unfortunately, in spite of all these good inten-tions, when the Bessemer made its maiden crossing a century ago, the

An end view of the *Castalia* in Dover Harbour.

speed was far below specification, the gyroscope would not work, and no sailor could operate the hydraulic gear efficiently by hand, so that the hoped-for swinging saloon never swung.

At the same time as the development of the *Bessemer* a rival craft was launched which was also intended to annihilate sea-sickness on the cross-Channel journey. This was the *Castalia*, designed with twin hulls and of exceedingly low draught, drawing only six feet of water, a decrease of eighteen inches on the draught of the Channel packet of that time, which it was hoped would enable the ship to operate at all states of the tide. The *Castalia* was designed by Captain Dicey, formerly a port officer at Calcutta, and his notion was based on the practice he had observed in India of steadying boats in a heavy swell by putting out two outriggers and securing a massive log to the ends of the outriggers. In Dicey's design each hull was intended to act as outrigger to the other. On the twin hulls he built a large flat-bottomed body-structure rigidly connected by girders to the floating framework. The vessel was large – 290 feet in length with a sixty-feet beam – and it allowed the provision of four large saloons, of which the two biggest were sixty feet by thirty-six, along with cabins, retiring-rooms and lavatories, and galleys which could serve the capacious dinners that were then expected by voyagers, weather permitting. But these sections of the accommodation were mere ante-rooms compared with his 'Crystal Palace' *pièce de résistance*, a grand saloon 160 feet long and sixty feet wide, roofed by a deck fourteen feet above the sea: the low level of this maindeck illustrates the optimism with which the stability of the *Castalia* was regarded. The paddles of the steamer were placed in the waterway between the hulls, and it was expected that the engines would allow a speed of nearly fifteen knots. But on her trials the *Castalia*'s speed was too low, the boilers inadequate, and her single virtue was the fact that she was comparatively steady.

THREE
TUNNELS AND BRIDGES

IN 1872 THE ENGLISH Channel Tunnel Company was formed, a detailed engineering scheme was projected, and eventually tunnelling
operations were begun which were advanced to a stage, a century ago,
when 2000 yards of tunnel had been bored below the sea from Shake-
speare's Cliff near Dover, and a similar distance towards England had
been achieved from Sangratte, near Calais. The comparative ease with
which the Channel Tunnel scheme was accepted resulted from the great
prestige deservedly earned by the promoters and engineers of the Mont
Cenis Tunnel which had been opened in the year before the formation of
the company, in 1871, between Savoy in France and Piemonte in Italy.
The decision to attempt the Mont Cenis Tunnel was, in turn, the result
of the development of a new rock-boring machine worked by compressed
air and using chisels made of a very hard steel. Eventually, therefore,
the enterprise owed its existence to man's increasing mastery over the
working of iron and the development of steel.

Mont Cenis is an alpine peak rising to a height of nearly 12,000 feet
and there is a pass some 7000 feet high. Hannibal marched his army
of 100,000 men and fifty elephants over this pass in 218 B.C. for
the attack on Rome. Napoleon built a carriage road over the pass
between 1802 and 1810. This was a precarious route into Italy for half a
century – not only hazardous because of the accidents that occurred to
the primitive coaches called *diligences* as their seven horses toiled up –
and, more dangerously, down – the incessant fortified zig-zags of the
route, but more hazardous because the conductors of the diligences,
holding the monopoly of the transport, virtually made a contract with
the travellers under which the money was paid down first and the

The Sommeiller Boring Machine.

conductor provided wayside board and lodgings under conditions where whatever he offered had to be accepted. The coming of the railways in Europe forced indignation at this frontier-ordeal to crisis point. If a tunnel could be built of sufficient width to take a train, the passenger could sit in his own seat with unpilfered luggage and thumb his nose at the diligence jarveys as he passed. The enterprise was proposed, and a careful survey was made. The points chosen on either side of the mountain were about seven and a half miles apart and three quarters of a mile above sea level. The summit of the 9500-foot rock under which they were mining would be a further mile above them. Because of the configuration of the mountain it was quite impossible to do what had been done in all the successful 'difficult' tunnels excavated so far in the century. It was out of the question to sink shafts to the level of the proposed tunnel so that boring could be carried out simultaneously at a number of points on that level. The work would have to be done from the two external exits only. This would mean an enormous increase in the time taken and great expense in ventilating some three miles of gallery on each side so that workmen could operate speedily without being affected by the fumes following each explosive blast. The duration of the operation was the most critical factor, since the longer the task took the more the labour costs would rise and the more delayed would be any prospect of profit. The situation was dramatically altered by an announcement by a French firm of engineers called Sommelier that they had developed a compressed air machine capable of automatically working special chisels known as 'jumpers' which could penetrate the hardest rock. This claim was immediately tested and found to be justified. The decision to undertake the Mont Cenis Tunnel was arrived at within weeks, and work was actually started in the same year – 1857 – although it was known that it would be years before sufficient of the new machines would be available and that much other machinery for ventilation and transport within the tunnel would have to be ordered and manufactured. After a renewed survey to achieve the greatest possible accuracy, the tunnelling was begun at either end using ordinary hand labour with picks and shovels in 1857, the same year as the scheme was decided on.

The northern end of the tunnel was proposed to be at Fourneaux, a place 3801 feet high. The southern end was to be at Bardonnêche, which was 4236 feet high. These heights were important, even to the

The journey across Mont Cenis.

inch, for from them all the surveying triangulations had to be made to distances of up to eight miles in order to fix the precise lines of the two tunnels advancing to meet each other, so that in fact they did meet each other and not pass by in the centre of the mountain. For four years manual labour was the only means of tunnelling and clearing. The tunnel went forward at a rate of some two feet a day from either side. In 1861 the machinery came up, but particularly at the southern end there were breakages and malfunctions both in the drills and the machines that operated them. The machines were in use for roughly only half the number of available days, and when they were in operation they were advancing at a slower rate than the former manual work. But after consistent on-the-spot repair and improvement the machines were in operation for 325 working days in 1862, and scored an average rate of advance of nearly four feet a day. Mechanical difficulties were even greater at the other end, where the problems of the air-compressing machinery were greater, and it was 1863 before the work was reliably regular.

A particular feature of the process was that the jumpers – the chisels so called because they were repeatedly 'shot' by the propellant into the rock with a slight turn of the chisel between each impact – were worked by compressed air which had been forced to 90 pounds a square inch by a method which harnessed the natural heads of water found within the mountain: a most ingenious use of a mountain spring. The escape of the compressed air not only ventilated the tunnels after the explosive charges but considerably cooled the galleries, which otherwise would have been almost impossible to work in what with the sweat, the naked lights and the gunpowder explosions. The Sommelier machines automatically propelled a chisel into the rock at a rate of three hundred blows a minute, turning the chisel slightly at each shot to duplicate the action of an auger or modern drill. Water was constantly forced into the holes to remove the debris. A number of these machines were mounted on one wheeled frame running on a tramway laid along the gallery. Each perforator could be angled in an individual direction and carried its own water jet to clear the debris. The holes were driven into the rock for a depth of about two and a half feet. If the points of the jumpers did not break – and this was a common enough occurrence since much of the rock was hard slatey limestone interspersed with veins of quartz, which apart from diamond was the hardest mineral then known – the operation

[43]

The Diamond Drill machinery for deep boring.

of boring thirty inches took up to fifty minutes. The cylinders were then shifted and a fresh series of boring started until about eighty holes had been made. The workers then disconnected the flexible tubes conveying compressed air and water to the Sommelier borers, the machines were stowed away, and the frames backtracked down the tramway. Specialist workers then wiped out the holes, charged them with gunpowder, and fired slow-burning fuses before hurrying to get behind strong wooden barricades erected a considerable distance off. After the explosion compressed air was siphoned in to clear the smoke and gas, and workmen pushed wagons up the tramway to carry away the detached stone. On a good sequence the boring would take seven hours, the priming and explosion one hour and the clearance four hours, so that a double series of operations could be completed in a twenty-four hour cycle, advancing the tunnel from each end by well over five feet, since the blasting weakened more than the depth of rock to which the boring holes had penetrated.

The rate of progress steadily quickened with improved methods and the skill gained from experience. At the end of 1864, when the machines had been in operation for little more than three years, it was calculated that the opening of the tunnel might be expected eleven years later, in 1875. In fact it was on Christmas Day of 1870 that perforator Number 45 bored a hole from Italy into France by piercing the wall of rock, about four yards thick, which separated one working from the other. An astonishing feat of engineering calculation was demonstrated when it was found that the centre lines of the two workings varied by one foot longitudinally, the line of the northern approach being higher than the southern by that interval, but in their horizontal directions they exactly agreed: all this after working physically blind for thirteen years through nearly eight miles. The actual length of the tunnel was found to be fifteen yards longer than had been calculated, being seven miles and 1059 yards. With amazing speed the tunnel was tidied, foundations prepared, the railway line laid with the necessary lay-bys and signalling apparatus, and the Mont Cenis Tunnel was opened in 1871.

Once the eventual success of this pioneer tunnel was assured, before its opening, the French and British entrepreneurs interested in constructing the Channel Tunnel resumed their planning with fresh vigour and commissioned the best engineers in Great Britain and France to draw up a feasibility analysis. Many of the engineers concerned had given years of thought to the project previously. This professional committee established that the Straits of Dover had not opened by a sudden disruption of the earth at that point but had been produced naturally and slowly by the gradual washing away of the upper chalk. This was an important conclusion since it rejected any supposition that there had been any volcanic upheaval or fissure in the sea-bed, which would have produced incalculable difficulties in boring, but that the geological formations beneath the Straits were identical with the formations of the two shores, and in fact a continuation of these strata. Mr Low, the principal British engineer engaged, took note of the new techniques used in the Mont Cenis Tunnel, where no intermediate shafts could be sunk; and although the proposed Channel Tunnel was to be three times as long as the alpine pioneer he recommended that no shafts should be sunk in the sea, as had been suggested earlier, but that preliminary vertical borings should be sunk in each shore and that small parallel galleries should be driven out from each country, with transverse connections, so that a preliminary system of ventilation could be installed as was then the practice in the coal mines of the time. Mr Low, on behalf of the committee, laid his plans before the Emperor Napoleon III in April 1867, and a working committee of French and British magnates was set up to further the project.

A very valuable aid to the work of this committee was the engineering analysis which had already been prepared by Sir John Hawkshaw, who had been concerned with the building of Holyhead harbour and several docks as well as part of the London Underground Railway, and who later constructed the Severn Tunnel. Hawkshaw had already made an elaborate study of a possible submarine tunnel to connect the railway systems of Great Britain and Europe. He had already initiated borings both at St Margaret's Bay near the South Foreland and at a point on the French coast three miles west of Calais, and had put down divers to examine the Channel bottom. He had established that the depth of chalk at the English coast was 470 feet below high water, and it was 750 feet below high water at the French coast. He had determined that, using artificial ventilation to disperse the fumes of the locomotives of the time, the Channel Tunnel could equally well take the form of a double track of railway lines or two single-line tunnels. With this unimpeachable information, the committee appointed by the Emperor of the French reported in 1869 that there was a continuity and regularity of

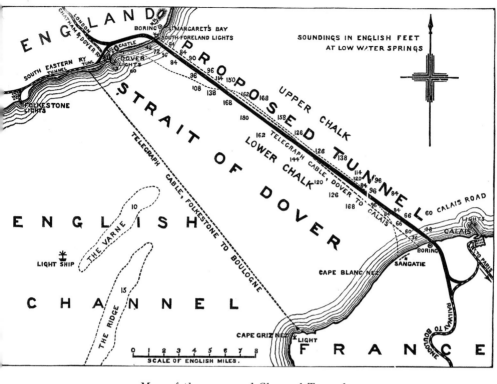

Map of the proposed Channel Tunnel.

Section of the proposed Channel Tunnel.

level in the grey chalk which constituted the lower stratum of the bed of the Channel, and that the proposition to drive a submarine tunnel through the lower part of this layer presented reasonable chances of success, barring unforeseen contingencies. The principal dangers would be some unlikely treacherous variation in the composition of the grey chalk or an influx of water through faults in the chalk. But they concluded that since grey chalk was comparatively soft – and indeed it was putty compared with the quartz and other hard rock that was being encountered under the Mont Cenis – the work of excavation would be relatively fast and easy and 'the execution of a tunnel, under the conditions of the project, is but a matter of time and money.'

The depth of water in the Channel along the proposed line of the Tunnel nowhere exceeded 180 feet – little more than half the height of St Paul's Cathedral – and the Tunnel was planned to run at least 200 feet below the bottom, rising towards each end with a moderate gradient. By 1875 the whole enterprise seemed a highly practical proposition, and the Victorians were already girding their loins to celebrate this new wonder of the age – 'This great project which bids fair to become a sober fact.' 'A tunnel under twenty miles of stormy sea seemed very much like an engineer's dream,' enthused the *Daily News* in January that year,

and it is only within the last few years that it has been regarded as a feasible project. Of its possibility, however, there seems now to be no manner of doubt. It is merely a stream of sea-water, and not a fissure in the earth, which divides us from the Continent. Prince Metternich was right in speaking of it as a ditch . . . The method by which it is proposed that the excavation should be made is in some respects similar to that which was successfully employed in tunnelling the Alps. Mont Cenis was pierced by machinery adapted to the cutting of hard rock; the chalk straits under the Channel are to be bored by an engine, invented by Mr Dickenson Brunton, which works in the comparatively soft strata like a carpenter's auger. A beginning will be made simultaneously on both sides of the Channel, and the effort will at first be limited to making a clear hole through from end to end. This small bore, or driftway, will be some seven or nine feet in diameter. If such a communication can be successfully made, the enlargement will be comparatively easy. Mr Brunton's machine is said to cut through chalk at the rate of a yard an hour. We believe that those which were used in the Mont Cenis Tunnel cut less than a yard a day of the hard rock of the mountain. Two years, therefore, ought to be sufficient to allow the workers from one end to shake hands with those from the other side. The enlargement of the driftway into the

[48]

completed tunnel would take four years' more labour and as many millions of money. The millions, however, would be easily raised if the driftway is made, since the victory will be won as soon as the two headways meet under the sea. The opening of such a communication between this country and the Continent will be a pure gain to the commercial and social interests of both sides. It obliterates the Channel so far as it hinders direct communication, yet keeps it intact for all those advantages of severance from the political complications of the Continent, which no generation has more thoroughly appreciated than our own. The commercial advantages of the communication must necessarily be beyond all calculation. A link between the two chief capitals of Western Europe, which should annex our railway system to the whole of the railways of the Continent, would practically widen the world to pleasure and travel and every kind of enterprise. The 300,000 travellers who cross the Channel every year would probably become three millions if the sea were practically taken out of the way by a safe and quick communication under it. The Channel Tunnel is the crowning enterprise of an age of vast engineering works. Its accomplishment is to be desired from every point of view, and, should it be successful, it will be as beneficent in its results as the other great triumphs of the science of our time.

But the English military authorities vetoed the Channel Tunnel. All that remains of it is what was there a century ago – 2000 yards of tunnel bored out from either side. The only questionable boon that ever came from 'this great project which bids fair to become a sober fact' is the discovery, by accident during the investigatory borings, of a coal field near Dover.

When in 1973 the British Government revived the Channel Tunnel project and arranged the finance of the whole scheme (which was pretty speedily abandoned) to complete the Tunnel by 1980 at a cost overall of £846 million, there was much talk of an alternative scheme to build a Channel Bridge. This proposal, said to be practical in the twentieth century, was not an idea which had occurred to the Victorian dreamers, although the nineteenth century had produced many outstanding examples of bridge-building which were sincerely admired as Victorian wonders. The great burst of bridge-building was in fact another aspect of the new discoveries regarding the working of iron. The earliest bridges over rivers or chasms were simple constructions of timber which, because of the nature of the material, could not last long. Bridges of boats or pontoons had been built, often as an emergency military measure as when Xerxes and his army crossed the Hellespont in this manner in 450

[49]

B.C. Suspension bridges had been used in the time of the ancient Chinese civilisation and were of course utilised, sometimes in the very primitive form of woven tendrils of vegetation, not only by unsophisticated tribes in central Africa but by the Incas of South America, where an Inca bridge of 200 feet span was encountered in Peru in the sixteenth century. But it was the Romans who, by their skilled use of the arch of stone, became the world's great bridge-builders, and some of their constructions, particularly the aqueducts, have lasted two thousand years. Stone and brick was the established medium for bridge-building until in 1796 the first notable bridge made of cast iron was erected over the river Wear at Sunderland. But cast iron was not a favourable material for building bridges for the simple reason that bridges are horizontal structures rather than vertical. Cast iron will withstand enormous crushing pressure but has a low elasticity or tensile strength, and it was tensile strength that was required rather than uncrushability: if a plank is suspended across two barrels and a man jumps up and down on the middle of it, it is relatively unimportant if the plank does not bruise under the man's heels but highly important if it snaps in two because, in effect, the man is extending the length of the plank by forcing it into a curve which the wood has not the elasticity to absorb. Consequently when new manufacturing techniques made wrought iron available in considerable quantity and in pieces of increased size, wrought iron was speedily adopted for bridge-building. Wrought iron had in the nineteenth century some four times the tensile strength of cast iron (though only a third of its resistance to crushing), and wrought iron wire, which was used in massive diameters for suspension bridges, had five times the tensile strength of cast iron.

It was in fact a suspension bridge, though not one utilising wire, that became the first famous wrought iron bridge in nineteenth century Britain. A suspension bridge is in effect a comparatively flat platform hung by ties of various lengths from the links of two chains suspended in mid-air from tall columns with the ends of the chain firmly anchored to the earth. Thomas Telford, the great Scottish civil engineer who built the Ellesmere and the Caledonian canals, and a thousand miles of road and 1200 bridges in Scotland alone, undertook the commission to re-engineer the whole of the London-to-Holyhead road. In order to make a complete job of it he proposed to throw a bridge across the Menai Straits from Caernarvonshire to Anglesey. He completed the project within

The Britannia Bridge, Menai Straits.

Section of a tube in the Britannia Bridge, Menai Straits.

6½ years at a cost of £120,000 and it was opened in 1825. For the main suspension columns he built two piers of Anglesey marble rising 153 feet above high-water level and distanced 580 feet apart: the total length of the bridge is 1710 feet. The main chains hanging from the columns droop 43 feet from their point of suspension, and so can almost be touched from the centre of the roadway, which is 102 feet above high water and was built by Telford to a width of 28 feet. (The bridge was reconstructed in 1940.) The chains were formed of flat wrought iron bars, nine feet long, 3¼ inches broad and one inch thick. Telford put sixteen main chains into the suspension, and formed each link of five bars joined by cross-bolts three inches in diameter. The main chains were connected by eight transverse stays in the form of cast iron tubes through which passed wrought iron bolts.

The other great bridge over the Menai Straits, the Britannia Bridge which carries the railway to Holyhead, established not only the superiority of wrought iron over cast iron but also the new system of the girder which had been developed for work in iron. It was designed by Robert Stephenson, the railway-engineer son of George, who did in fact help his father with the construction of the *Rocket* locomotive. But the girder system used for the Britannia Bridge was invented by Sir William Fairbairn, an expert in iron and a pioneer in the construction of iron ships. The principle of the girder is basically that the weight of a beam can be lightened by reducing the material in its horizontal centre line, where it is under no strain, so that a concentration of strength (which is allied to mass and weight) can be applied to the lower section, which takes most stress, and to the upper section, which takes a proportion of the stress. Fairbairn developed this idea to produce the box girder, which as he refined it in the Britannia Bridge became a hollow rectangular tube with the train running along the centre of the tube. Stephenson chose a site on the Straits about a mile south of Telford's bridge where a rock projected from the bed of the sea, rising about ten feet above low water and being submerged by ten feet at high water. On this he built a central tower, a massive erection 62 feet by 52 feet in area and well over 200 feet high. On the shore line at either side, 460 feet from the central tower, he built supporting towers and continued the run-up of the rail track towards the land for a further section of 176 feet each side protected by a stone embankment and most of it still carrying the girder tubes. Since each of the two railway tracks runs in its own separate tube, the

[53]

The Albert Bridge, Saltash.

total length of continuous tube for either direction was in fact 1513 feet. The rails rested on longitudinal timber sleepers secured by angle-irons to the ribs of the lower framing and secured by two million rivets hammered in red-hot by a then novel process so that on contraction the plates and the ribs had very firm adhesion. The total weight of each continuous tube before the rails were set in was 5250 tons. The four great 460-feet middle sections were built on the shore, floated out on pontoons, and raised by hydraulic pressure, literally inch by inch with timber and masonry supports being built up for every inch gained, until they had reached their required height of 102 feet above the sea at the centre tower. In order to allow for expansion and contraction in different weather the tubes were set to rest on rollers of six inches diameter in the main towers and on gun-metal ball-bearings of six inches diameter at the shoreside abutments. Expansion and contraction in a single day was measured as up to three inches. The rigidity of the tubes was so strong that the heaviest train could deflect them only one inch downwards and the strongest gale one inch sideways. The bridge, which cost £600,000, was opened in October 1850.

Almost immediately the enterprising railway engineers set out to conquer an even more difficult proposition. The man concerned on this occasion was Brunel, who determined to extend the Great Western Railway from Plymouth into Cornwall by what we now know as the Saltash Bridge, though it was named the Albert Bridge when it was opened by the Prince Consort in 1860 shortly before his death. The space of water across the Tamar was almost the same as at the Menai Straits – 910 feet as against 920. The spot was more sheltered from gales than the Anglesey site, but the river was tidal and the central support had to be built, not on a rock ten feet below high water but on a mud-bank seventy feet down which extended for a further twenty feet in depth before a stratum of solid foundation was encountered. This could only be reached by building a wrought iron cylinder one hundred feet high and 37 feet across and lowering it on to the mud-bank. The cylinder cut through the mud by its own weight for a considerable depth before finally coming to rest. The water inside was then pumped out, and workmen went down to clear the mud and gravel by manual labour until they reached the bedrock. On this foundation a solid pillar of granite was built up inside the cylinder to a height above high-water level. The pillar was then extended with four iron columns, each a

[55]

hundred feet high. Masonry columns reaching to the same height were built at each shore to take the section of the track immediately above the water, and pillars of diminishing height ran back to the rail level on each side giving the bridge a total length of 2240 feet, of which 910 feet were actually over water. This main bridge structure was again designed in two spans of 455 feet each. The principle adopted was the double bow-string girder, giving the very attractive appearance of the harmonics diagram of a plucked string damped at the middle and vibrating with the octave of the fundamental note. The top arcs of the two spans were in fact, viewed in cross-section as well as from the side, wide ellipses. The bridge carried only one track, so that its width was only some sixteen feet, and the top bows are huge elliptical tubes with a horizontal diameter of 16 feet 10 inches and a vertical diameter of twelve feet. They are made of cast iron, whereas the bottom bow-strings are reverse arches of wrought iron, falling in the same manner as the chains of a suspension bridge, though this is not a suspension bridge. The level bearing the rails was suspended from both arcs of the bow-strings and carefully tied and strutted for rigidity. At its final test a train consisting entirely of heavy locomotives was driven on to the bridge, and the centre deflection was seven inches. As with the Britannia Bridge, the tubes were put into place by being built on shore, then loaded on to pontoons and raised into position by hydraulic power. The height of the track above water is 150 feet. The completion of the Saltash Bridge was a fitting climax to the life of Isambard Kingdon Brunel, whose reputation was to be so poignantly affected almost immediately. As has been said, his ambitiously designed ship the *Great Eastern* steamed out on her inauspicious maiden voyage in September 1859, eight days before he died. The Saltash Bridge was then in practical operation, though it was not formally opened until the next year, and he therefore died amid acclaim for the two projects, not knowing of the *Great Eastern's* initial failure and eventual success.

FOUR
THE SUEZ CANAL

IN THE MIDDLE of November 1875 an English journalist, travel-stale with the strain of a hurried journey from Paris, took a cab from Charing Cross to the Foreign Office and asked urgently to see an acquaintance who was an under-secretary there. The news he brought caused an instant flurry. The Prime Minister was immediately told of it, and quickly got in touch with City bankers. An emergency Cabinet was called and asked to approve a decision that could not be referred to Parliament, since it was not then sitting and in any case the publicity of open debate would have terminated the entire operation. Confidential enciphered cables were sent, and plenipotentiaries despatched with authority to sign, at an intermediate meeting-point, documents that could never be rescinded, for the payment of money that would never be reimbursed. On 25 November, ten days after the first revelation had been made, the Prime Minister wrote to Queen Victoria: 'It is just settled; you have it, Madam . . . Four millions sterling! . . . There was only one firm that could do it – Rothschilds. They behaved admirably; advanced the money at a low rate, and the entire interest of the Khedive is now yours, Madam: . . . Disraeli.'

'The entire interest of the Khedive' was nothing less than a controlling interest – seven-sixteenths of the shares in one block – of the Suez Canal. The Suez Canal project had been consistently opposed by British politicians and – with one honourable exception – by British engineers since its inception as a feasible operation in 1845. Prime Minister Palmerston had opposed it and Gladstone had cast cautious doubts on its practical potentiality, about which he knew nothing more than his experts told him, and its financial solidness, on which he was as,

Monsieur Ferdinand Lesseps.

theoretical as many other and more modern economists. Yet the scheme had gone through, on French capital in the main, and the canal had been opened in 1869. The ruler of Egypt was the Khedive (Viceroy) Ismail, owing nominal allegiance to Turkey, who was a relatively good administrator but totally unpractical as a financier. By the autumn of 1875 he found that he had either to find four million pounds within a fortnight or declare the public bankruptcy of his Government – a fate far worse than death a century ago, compared with the levity with which our statesmen now acknowledge our paper pauperage. He promptly began undercover negotiations to sell his Suez Canal stock to a consortium of French capitalists. The success of this operation would have given the French – still in the eyes of politicians our traditional enemies – a monopoly control of the canal. Since its opening Disraeli had become increasingly aware of the importance of the canal with regard to our commitments in India, where he was already planning that the Queen should be proclaimed Empress, and of the commercial profits as well as the military communications that had been notably facilitated by the canal passage which the British had so long opposed. The arguments for British condominium of the canal involved not only the situation in India but also British aspirations for the control of Egypt, which were in fact consolidated by our eventual control of the canal. All these considerations of imperial power and prestige were brought to an urgent climax when the British journalist loyally spilled the beans to the Foreign Office in November 1875. Disraeli made his gentleman's agreement with Rothschilds – the only organisation which could provide ready cash in the short time available – and subsequently persuaded Parliament without the least difficulty that he had ensured reasonable rates for the armada of British shipping that was already using the canal, and staked a substantial interest in the future of Egypt, which indeed after many years of de facto domination became a British protectorate in 1904.

The idea of a Suez Canal connecting the Mediterranean with the Red Sea was not new. There is evidence that a primitive canal making this junction was cut in 1380 B.C. Napoleon seriously considered a modern canal, but cancelled the project when he was told that the Red Sea was 33 feet higher than the Mediterranean – an obstacle which a couple of locks could have overcome. In 1833 a Catholic priest, Father Enfantin, enthusiastically advocated the project and gained the attention of

Mehemet Ali, the Albanian who had ruled as governor of Egypt for forty years, and Ferdinand de Lesseps, the French vice-consul in Cairo. Surveys were carried out, but abandoned because of outbreaks of the plague. But de Lesseps and the ruler maintained their interest, and in 1846 the Société d'Etude du Canal du Suez was formed. This society commissioned the investigations of a number of internationally respected engineers, including the British Robert Stephenson. Stephenson, a railway engineer, thought the canal scheme totally impractical and recommended as an alternative the construction of a railway throughout the depth of Egypt, and a line connecting Alexandria and Suez was built. De Lesseps, however, persisted. He gained the support of another British engineer, John (later Sir John) Hawkshaw, who was later to be a vigorous proponent of the Channel Tunnel, and Hawkshaw's expert advice was decisive. Mehemet Ali had died at the age of eighty and the Khedive was his great-grandson when, in 1854, de Lesseps formed the Compagnie Universelle du Canal Maritime de Suez. The work was started in 1856, and almost immediately international opposition to it seemed to have doomed it.

It had been designed that the canal should be built by forced labour supplied by the Khedive Said. 'The fellahin were to be induced,' said a contemporary, 'by a liberal supply of stick to give their labour for a miserable pittance of rice.' *Corvée*, or forced labour, was a Roman and later a mediaeval institution which had notably been continued in France, where, although its excesses had undoubtedly contributed to the French Revolution, it was maintained in a revised form until after the building of the Suez Canal; and in Egypt the Nile barrage was constructed by forced labour between 1841 and 1867. Nevertheless it was understood among European statesmen that, although the Egyptian peasant might cheerfully work on a scheme of general benefit to bring sweet water from the Nile to other dry and thirsty places in Egypt, to be obliged to work at a waterway of salt water which was only to be of use to foreigners who passed through their country could not be expected of frail human beings. The spokesmen of the frail, who, it is interesting to note, styled themselves even in 1856 as the representatives of the free countries, declared that the cruelties involved in the forced labour scheme equalled the horrors of other slave countries. This is said to have been one of the reasons why Lord Palmerston opposed the canal scheme. His argument was not only that the *corvée* was injurious to the health

[60]

and expectation of life of the Egyptians, but that one of the conditions under which the French company had been allowed to begin the project was that it should be executed by free labour.

Pressure was therefore put on the Sultan of Turkey, the nominal over-lord of Egypt, and he placed a veto on the use of forced labour. For de Lesseps this was a blessing in disguise. He later declared that if he had depended on the forced labour of the fellahin he could never have sur-mounted the gigantic difficulties implicit in the task. He was compelled to turn his attention to more modern methods, particularly the machines recently adopted for dredging the Thames and the Clyde, and he stated that as a result the work was done in half the time and at half the expense that would have been necessary if he had relied on the native peasantry. These dredging machines were held at readiness while a rough trough was dug out by spades to a depth of about twelve feet. Water was then let in and the steam-dredges were floated down stream, moored along the bank, and set to work. There were two sorts of dredges, the operation of which is common enough now but was a marvel at the time. The shore-dredger was a broad flat-bottomed barge on which stood a high framework of wood supporting an endless chain of heavy iron buckets. The chain was turned by steam, and the height of the axle was varied progressively so that the empty buckets, revolving on the chain, always struck the bottom of the canal at a fixed angle. They emerged full of mud and sand and water, and at the top of the revolution they discharged their contents into a long open trough running at right angles to the barge. The end of the trough projected for some yards inland of the bank, and the stream of mud and water was continually raising the height of the embankment. These vessels were supplemented by the mid-stream dredgers which emptied the contents of their buckets into barges moored alongside, the barges being squarely loaded with railway trucks. When each barge was full it was steered to the bank, where a steam crane lifted the individual trucks on to rails at the waterside. The rails were set at an upward incline over the bank and drawn to the top by an endless rope. At the peak of the embankment a bolt was pulled, the side of the truck fell open, and the mud was shot on to the land. The empty truck returned to the elevator platform by another set of rails, and was lowered back into the barge from which it had come. The spectacle of this smoking and steaming and unutter-ably noisy operation in the heart of a desert panorama excited many observers, one of whom wrote: 'The sensation of wonder at the prodigious scale of the operations in progress increases day by day as one moves along what seems to be a wide river, with villages on the banks, and smoky funnels and white sails on the surface. The hydraulic machines, which groan and snort and rattle their chains as they work, are of enormous size; and though each of them seems to be pouring forth a volume of mud, yet the mind finds it hard to believe that all of these together can lift up and throw over the banks enough to make any appreciable progress between yesterday and today. The sand dredged from below is either carried out to sea in barges, or (farther inland) is delivered in a stream from a lofty iron tube, 220 feet long, with its mouth over one bank, or it is hoisted up an iron inclined plane and cast upon the shore, until the heap on each side of the water is fifty feet high. The engines for this purpose are forty in number, and each of them cost £40,000. The expenses at present amount to £200,000 every month, and the work has already absorbed eight millions sterling.' The total cost of the operation was in fact twelve millions, and Disraeli did a very good deal when he bought almost half of the equity for four millions.

The northern outlet of the canal, on to the Mediterranean, was constructed at Port Said, a notorious name in later Victorian times when all the P. & O. liners stopped there and the full felony of a transit port was exercised to the detriment and dubious pleasure of the travellers who passed through. At the outset of the enterprise Port Said had been a village of about one hundred inhabitants. But a century ago, before it had got into its full stride of infamy, it held six thousand people, all exploiting to the full the character of the frontier town which in fact it was. 'Like all the other towns on the Suez route,' said a traveller who had suffered there, 'it has a striking resemblance to the newly settled cities of America, and being composed of very combustible materials, would be burnt down in a very short space of time.' One has the impression that the writer of this description was regretfully short of matches. Port Said had docks, quays and warehouses, and its harbour stretched two miles out to sea with the protection of two breakwaters constructed of concrete blocks, ten tons each in weight, erected on the model of the water defences built in Holland where, as in Egypt, stone was hard to come by. In the early days of the canal its entrance was marked by two imposing obelisks the construction of which also indicated that nobody had robbed the pyramids of any stone. They had been erected as

[62]

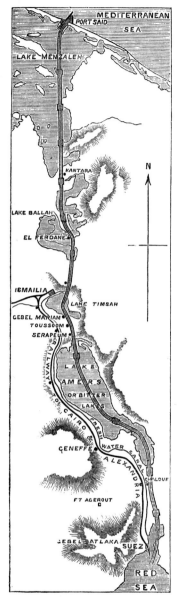

Contemporary map of the Suez Canal.

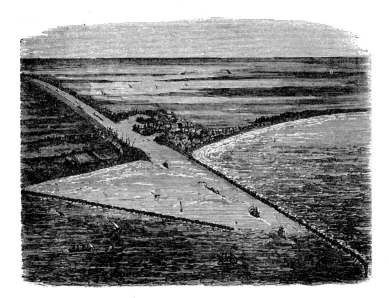

View of Port Said.

A breakwater at Port Said.

part of the monumental decorations put up for the official opening of the canal by the Empress Eugénie of France. But they consisted merely of a facing of canvas on a framework of wood, in the hopeful expectation that at some future time there would be a shipment of granite.

From Port Said the canal ran due south through the swamp called Lake Menzaleh, a 28-mile stretch which had been the hardest of all to complete because of the shifting bottom of this muddy lagoon. There was nothing spectacular here to show for all the pains of construction, and the difficulty of making a solid foundation for the sand-banks of the canal course through a very long stretch of brackish water, and ensuring that both sides of the embankment were leakproof although the passing ships put up a considerable wash, could be little appreciated from the deck-chair of a passenger liner. What was attractive from such a view-point were the enormous number of white duck swimming in and flying about their habitation here, and the white pelicans which stalked through the marshy places. In the humid air above the wide waters of this lagoon the mirage effect was also seen to best advantage. The land and swamp in this area was indeed so flat that even Port Said could not be distinguished three miles out at sea, in spite of the Empress's obelisks. At the southern end of Lake Menzaleh on the neck of land dominated by the town of Kantara there had been the traditional caravan highway on the trade route from Cairo to Syria. With the coming of the canal it was now necessary to provide a floating bridge to take the camel trains across. At Kantara there was stationed an Egyptian man-o'-war to police the canal, and in the town itself, a disgruntled chronicler reported, 'there are two hotels which condescend to supply the traveller at exorbitant prices'. South of Kantara there was a fifteen-mile stretch, also proceeding dead south, down the neck of land and through Lake Ballah: a section where it had also been necessary to construct sand embankments within a mere but, since Lake Ballah was virtually dry, there had been no difficulties comparable with the northern stretch.

The southerly end of Lake Ballah was marked by the village of El Ferdane, and the next section – five miles across land to Lake Timsah – was the stretch where the work had originally been started by the forced labour of the Egyptian fellahin which had aroused so much opposition in Europe. This part of the canal had, however, been completed by them, a great army of 60,000 peasants with the comparatively tiny Eastern spades which have always appeared ludicrous to Irish navvies, organised into bustling gangs of whom 35,000 worked in the day time and 25,000 at night. A tramway had been laid down, and the sand was taken in ballast trucks and shot into the desert. Lake Timsah, at the southern end of this section, had diminished over the centuries into a broad and barren sandy hollow by the time the canal engineers prospected it. It contained only the relics of a few sandy pools, none of them deep enough to submerge a man. De Lesseps needed this space, however, as a canal reservoir, and as the excavation of the canal proceeded southward he in effect tapped the Mediterranean from 48 miles away and made of Timsah a real lake again, attractive to look at, about three miles in breadth, but filled now, as it had never been before, with salt sea water. On a northern curve of Lake Timsah the headquarters of the Suez Canal Company had been established, since the point was roughly equidistant from either end of the waterway and had communications by rail with both Cairo and Suez. Before the canal operation was started this spot had been merely a nomads' night-stop with a few tents as its only architecture. It became the important settlement of Ismailia, named after the Khedive, and the Viceroy himself determined to build a palace here. Other magnates began the construction of stone villas, there was a certain social life there because of the family quarters of the canal company officers, a hotel was built, and Ismailia promised to become a very attractive watering-place – which indeed it did as the years passed. Its great advantage was that it had a supply of fresh water brought from Cairo by the Sweet Water Canal, and a description of the settlement by a contemporary Scottish writer illustrates not only the character of the place but also the hardy conditions which British travellers of the time cheerfully accepted as a kind of sporting adventure. 'The Sweet Water Canal is from thirty to forty feet wide, and boats with all sorts of cargoes are towed through it by men on foot, or sail along gaily if there is a breeze to fill their snowy wings. My canoe excited the greatest delight among all this river population, both when she skimmed over the water with her blue sails, or rested by the bank with her cabin rigged up, and my dinner cooked, and my little reading lamp and mosquito curtains arranged for the night. I managed to sleep thus in the canoe very comfortably, though the nights were cold; and on Lake Timsah a jackal paid me a visit at a very unfashionable hour by moonlight. During one day a violent gale swept across the canal. To look at the desert was to see a vast yellow picture of men and camels dimly floating in a sea of sand without any horizon. The quantity of sand whisked from the plain, and cast into the canal water by a wind like this, will be a serious matter to deal with. An ounce of sand per square yard amounts to 500 tons on the whole canal, and the wind sometimes blows in this way for a month together.'

Near the Viceroy's palace an area of beautiful gardens had been developed, watered by the sweet water irrigation, and one of the most attractive, with orange trees and tall acacias, enclosed the house of Ferdinand de Lesseps in the vicinity of his company headquarters. The breadth of Lake Timsah, carefully chosen but very luckily located as the half-way house for the Suez Canal, enabled a double channel to be constructed here, so that ships could pass each other safely by channels marked with buoys. (After the opening of the canal work went on continuously to widen it, and many other passing-places were constructed.) South-east of Lake Timsah, where the canal took a south-easterly course across a five-mile stretch of sand leading to the Bitter Lakes, the French engineer had come across his most formidable hazard. In this stretch the English-type dredgers had been used to float in after a preliminary channel had been hand-dug. But the line of the canal led directly to an unavoidable crop of rock, eighty feet in length and lying only twelve feet below the surface. This obstacle was discovered only a few months before the advertised time of the opening of the canal and threatened to throw the whole project off schedule. De Lesseps moored a large raft over the sunken rock and, lacking any mechanical boring tool, had workmen hand-drilling down at the rock with long poles carrying steel heads. Charges of gunpowder were packed in water-proof containers within the holes that had been drilled, and fired by an electric battery. The site of this rock was Serapeum, where an original canal had been dug by the Pharoah Seti I 3250 years before. From Serapeum the south-easterly line of the canal passed through the so-called Bitter Lakes. This had been an enormous area of sandy marsh containing very brackish water. The theoretical opponents of the canal scheme had always maintained that it would be impossible to keep this vast space filled with sea water. They said the water would either sink in the sand or be evaporated by the sun. Nothing of the sort occurred when, fourteen years after the operation had started, the Khedive Ismail cut the last embankment of the reservoir of the Plain of Suez and allowed the Red Sea to flow in to meet the Mediterranean. The only slight accident was that

[67]

Elevators and dredgers used in the construction of the Suez Canal.

the southern sea flowed in and up the canal into the Bitter Lakes with an unforeseen force that swept away a number of barriers intended to diminish its effect on the banks. But the Bitter Lakes filled and became a huge inland sea 25 miles long and from six to seven miles wide.

It was on the last stretch of the canal, through the sand from Chalouf at the south of the Bitter Lakes to the port of Suez itself, that both the mechanical and economical climax of the operation was seen to its best advantage and the final demonstration of the price of abandoning forced labour was made. The Scot who had been canoeing on the Sweet Water Canal and Lake Timsah paddled south along the extending line of the completed works and reported:

At Chalouf I found 14,000 men at work. They labour very hard indeed, running up the hill with baskets of sand on their heads. About 1000 donkeys walk in long lines with neat mat baskets on their backs. In curious and close contrast to these simple carriers the mighty power of steam toils and puffs as it hurls up huge bulks of heavy clay; and it is, perhaps, only in Egypt one could see such human and animal power exerted in such competition with steam power. The labourers are sent from all parts of Egypt. They must come, but they are highly paid – from two francs to three francs per day. Prices both of labour and food have risen very much since the canal has been begun, but the supply of fish has rapidly increased.

Enormous extra labour had been engaged also for the construction by the Suez Canal Company of vast docks well clear of the canal on the western coast of the Red Sea. The Cairo and Alexandria Railway was extended by two miles, carried through the sea on an embankment to service these docks and quays, so that passengers taking the overland route could board their ships for the east.

At the opening of the canal de Lesseps showed his confidence by allowing a flotilla of fifty ships to pass through from north to south, led by the Imperial Yacht *Aigle* carrying the Empress Eugénie, wife of Napoleon III. Thanks to the hand-drilling for the explosive charges at Serapeum, the operation was finished dead on schedule in November 1869. The only celebrant who was late was Giuseppe Verdi, who was writing the grand opera *Aida* for performance at the Cairo Opera House to mark the occasion. He could not finish the work, which of course has a valid Egyptian theme, and its first night did not occur until 1871. De Lesseps had his own celebration by marrying a comely young lady eight days after the opening and carrying her off to his villa at Ismailia.

Napoleon I's advisers, who had assured the Emperor in 1798 that the waters of the Red Sea were 33 feet higher than the Mediterranean, were proved wrong when the last sluice was cut at Suez. There was no eddy or fall at the point where the waters met. There is, however, a strong northerly current running up the canal from Suez and the tide in the Red Sea has a difference between high water and low water of seven feet, compared with the almost tideless Mediterranean. The tide was observed to run up the canal with great force but to die out in the vast area of the Bitter Lakes, where it became diffused and made no further effect on the northerly sections of the canal. After the Bitter Lakes became full the average temperature of inhabited locations on the banks fell by some five degrees Centigrade. The colour of the 'Red' Sea water is green, while that of the Mediterranean is more blue. It was found that the canal began to swarm with sea fish, but they kept to their respective ends of the water-way. This was probably not that the fish wanted nothing to do with strangers, but rather that the water at the northern end of the Bitter Lakes retained a very bitter quality and the fish had no inclination to pass this natural barrier.

The canal is roughly 103 miles long and when it was first cut it was on average 100 yards wide and 26 feet deep. (It is now 197 feet wide and 34 feet deep.) In 1869 it was said to have cut the route from London or Liverpool to Bombay from 10,000 miles to 5,000 miles. When Disraeli bought Britain into an enterprise with which she had formerly declined to be associated he was protecting the new short sea-route to India which at the time occupied far greater attention in imperial strategy than it did later. It also involved Great Britain in a near-century of trouble, since the country's commercial and military strength became artificially concentrated in a small area of great vulnerability which did in fact expose a channel of naval power to land attack and the threat of occupation in two world wars. The eventual nationalisation of the Suez Canal Company by an emergent Egypt was no great commercial crisis, since the Canal was to pass back wholly into Egyptian hands in 1968, 99 years after its opening.

De Lesseps always paid tribute to the Yorkshire engineer John Hawkshaw, whose favourable expert report on the project had swung the vacillating Khedive to make the final decision to go ahead with the scheme. At the opening of the canal he consistently introduced Hawkshaw to distinguished guests with the words 'This is the gentleman to whom I owe the canal.' Ferdinand de Lesseps, by birth a French vicomte, received not only the Grand Cross of the Légion d'Honneur for his work on the Suez Canal but also an English knighthood. He did not stay overlong at his Ismailia villa with his new bride, who became at astonishing speed the mother of twelve children. In 1881 de Lesseps went out to Panama, where he had already been working on a design for the Panama Canal, and construction was commenced. Work was stopped in 1888 when only a quarter of the channel was completed. But, although de Lesseps had originally estimated that the work would cost a total of £24 million, his company was already £74 million in debt. There had been some mismanagement, and a fearful drain into the hands of Colombian politicians and contractors on a scale which de Lesseps had been entirely unprepared to meet in a free country, after his comparatively easy ride with the despot Khedive Ismail. But what had struck the scheme most viciously was the recurrence of yellow fever and malaria. In the rumble of political scandal in France after the collapse of the Panama project, de Lesseps and his son (by his first marriage) were imprisoned on charges of fraud. He came out of prison a broken man and retired to England. Later he was exonerated of complicity in any fraud and he returned to France to die. The rights of the French Panama company were sold after his death to the United States Government. After the United States Army surgeon William Gorgas, with a corps of 2000 men, had begun the measures which were to eliminate the sources of the fever which had killed off the previous project, the Panama Canal, continuing the workings which de Lesseps had cut, began to be excavated in 1906 and was formally declared open in 1920. The Panama Canal is less than half the length of the Suez Canal, but ships have to pass through a series of locks because the water in the centre of the isthmus is kept at a higher level.

Walter machines in a newspaper's printing plant.

FIVE
COMMUNICATIONS

IT IS SHAMEFULLY EASY to laugh at an earlier epoch of our own civilisation from the superior heights of the knowledge gained in the age that followed it, and the sphere of communications is the easiest subject on which to provoke superior sniggering because it is in communications above everything else that the twentieth century seems to have shot ahead of the past. This is not in fact so. The nineteenth century may justly be claimed to have been more revolutionary than any preceding period *and than the epoch which followed it* as far as communications are concerned. For the nineteenth century made the discoveries and used them, while the twentieth century skilfully exploited what were for the most part inherited parcels of knowledge. Printing had hardly changed since Gutenberg and Caxton until fast printing was introduced in 1814. Electricity was known as a natural phenomenon like lightning, but the connection between magnetism and electricity was not established until 1820. Radiocommunication had never been heard of as a technical term a century ago, but it was in 1864 that Clerk Maxwell predicted the possibility of generating waves radiating into space from an oscillatory electric circuit, and in his *Theory of Electricity and Magnetism* published in 1873 he established the identity of electromagnetic and light-waves travelling at three hundred thousand million centimetres a second – and that work was the foundation of television and space travel. Therefore, when certain aspects of communication, as they were known a century ago, are narrated in this chapter the mood will not be of supercilious tolerance, even though some of the terms, like *the electric telegraph*, are quaint in themselves and wilfully used for comic effect today. They were genuine Victorian wonders, and any account of them should reflect the

[73]

genuine wonder which the Victorians felt for them and which indeed they should command in a later age which may be more slick but is not necessarily more sophisticated.

Printing, as has been said, had hardly changed as a craft for 350 years after the first Bible was printed in 1450, and the printing press was basically the same at the beginning of the nineteenth century as it had been when Caxton issued his *Dictes or Sayengis of the Philosophers* from his Westminster press on 18 November 1477. It was fundamentally a wooden press with screws which, with the ink wiped off, might have been used as a farmer's cheese press, and no substantial improvement had been made in its long history. In 1798 Charles, the third Earl Stanhope – who was an unlikely but valid chairman of the Revolution Society and an avowed republican after being a strong opponent of the British action against the infant United States in the American War of Independence – applied his revolutionary principles to the technique of printing and developed a press, the first in history, which was made of iron. He provided it with a combination of levers so that the platen, that is, the flat plate which overlays the paper and received the pressure, was forced down with great power at the moment when the paper came in contact with the type. Presses of his design could turn out 250 impressions an hour, and a century ago the very finest book-printing was still being done on presses of this design. It was 'hand-printing' where, in order to print with the greatest clearness and depth of colour, a much thicker ink was used which required more thorough application and spreading than a machine could achieve.

But Stanhope's press was useless for the rapid production of clean print which the newspapers needed for their then soaring circulations. In 1814 König set up for *The Times* of London two steam-driven machines which could produce 1100 newspapers an hour. *The Times*, on 28 November 1814, heralded this innovation as

The greatest improvement connected with printing since the discovery of the art itself. A system of machinery almost organic has been devised and arranged which, while it relieves the human frame of its laborious efforts in printing, far exceeds all human powers in rapidity and dispatch. That the magnitude of the invention may be justly appreciated by its effects, we shall inform the public that after the letters are placed by the compositors, and enclosed in what is called the 'form', [*now spelt in the printing trade* forme, *the body of type secured in an iron frame for printing at one impression*] little more remains for man to do than to attend upon and watch this unconscious agent in its operations. The machine is then merely supplied with paper, itself places the form, inks it, adjusts the paper to the form newly inked, stamps the sheet, and gives it forth to the hands of the attendant, at the same time withdrawing the form for a fresh coat of ink, which itself again distributes, to meet the ensuing sheet now advancing for impression, and the whole of these complicated acts is performed with such a velocity and simultaneousness of movement that no less than 1,100 sheets are impressed in one hour. That the completion of an invention of this kind, not the effect of chance, but the result of mechanical combinations, methodically arranged in the mind of the artist, should be attended with many obstructions and much delay may be readily admitted. Our share in this event has, indeed, only been the application of the discovery, under an agreement with the patentees, to our own particular business; yet few can conceive, even with this limited interest, the various disappointments and the deep anxiety to which we have for a long course of time been subjected. Of the person who made the discovery we have little to add. Sir Christopher Wren's noblest monument is to be found in the building which he erected; so is the best tribute of praise which we are capable of offering to the inventor of the printing machine comprised in the preceding description, which we have feebly sketched, of the powers and utility of his invention. It must suffice to say further, that he is a Saxon by birth, that his name is König, and that the invention has been executed under the direction of his friend and countryman, Bauer.

The long-winded assignment of the credit to König and Bauer has some quality of the nineteenth century journalists who were paid a penny a line for their freelance contributions and therefore spun the words out to their greatest prolixity. The König machine was, of course, revolutionary but there were obvious improvements immediately necessary. The paper was printed only on one side of the sheet, and the sheets had therefore to be passed through again to the other of the two machines installed to be 'perfected', or printed on the other side. A modification of the machine by Applegarth and Cowper enabled the sheets to be perfected in the same machine. The adapted invention was a major revolution in printing, and there stemmed from it the genuinely cheap books and newspapers which did so much to advance the culture of Victorian times. But it will have been noted that *sheets* of paper were still required, and each sheet had to be handled, being pushed into the machine by a man called the feeder, or layer-on. As communication by railway and telegraph became speedier, with the practical effect that news was pouring into newspaper offices from their sources and correspondents faster than they could send it out in printed form, the necessity of faster printing became paramount. A greater speed was required than could be obtained from any flat forme press. For in this method of printing the heavy table containing the type had to be moved, stopped, moved back and again stopped during the printing of a single sheet. The shocks and strains which the machine received during these reversals of direction imposed an impassable limit on the speed with which sheets could be printed. Applegarth, therefore, being appealed to by *The Times* to produce a machine capable of working off a faster delivery of impressions, abandoned the flat bed and the reciprocal motion and adopted a rotary revolution of the type forme.

This had become possible through the enterprise of a man called Nicholson who had devised the system of building type with the individual letters in a wedge shape, which enabled the pieces of metal to fit exactly round the drum of a cylinder and still 'marry', without excessive space between the letters, when the external diameter of the type on the cylinder fanned out. But, though the method showed a possibility, it was uneconomic in practice. Applegarth therefore used ordinary type, set up on flat surfaces forming the sides of a prism corresponding to the circumference of his revolving type cylinder, which was very large and placed vertically. The flat surfaces which received the type were the width of the columns of the newspaper, and the type formes were firmly locked up by screwing down wedge-shaped rules between the columns at the angles of the polygon. These formed the column rules making the upright lines between the columns, and by their shape they secured the type in place. The forme was attached to a cylinder of five feet six inches diameter, but the type occupied only a portion of its circumference, the remainder serving as an inking table. Round the great cylinder were eight impression rollers, each with a set of inking rollers. At each turn of the great cylinder eight sheets received the impression. It was still necessary to apply paper in sheets but these sheets were carried up automatically and vertically. With this machine up to 12,000 impressions could be struck off in an hour, and when *The Times* produced a monster edition announcing the death of the Duke of Wellington, printing for 14 November 1852, 70,000 copies were printed in one day without any stoppage to wash the rollers or brush the formes. But the vertical machine was outdated when the last great printing invention of the era was made. This was the discovery of a method of producing at speed a stereotype plate from a forme of type. A thick wad consisting of moist sheets of unsized paper, pasted together and compressed into layers, was forced down with great pressure on the forme of type. The *papier mâché* accurately received the negative impression of the type. It was put while still flexible on the inside surface of an iron semi-cylinder and molten metal was poured between the *papier mâché* and the cylinder which was the core of the whole operation. The metal hardened to become a half-cylinder of type, usually one page in area. Two semi-cylinders were put on one roller bearing the type of, say, pages 1 and 24 of the newspaper, and two other semi-cylinders carried the type of pages 2 and 23. The Walter machine – the printing machine, actually patented by MacDonald and Calverley but named Walter in honour of the proprietor of *The Times*, which printed from these stereotype plates – produced an impression of four pages of the paper, printed on both sides, but not printed in sheets. The paper was now fed from a huge roll and the product was automatically cut into sheets after printing and then laid in piles. This system added greatly to the speed of production and was also markedly economical in manpower since it dispensed with the labour of the highly-skilled layers-on. Not only *The Times* but many other newspapers used the Walter Press. Later it was challenged by the rotary machine invented by the American Colonel Richard Hoe, who set up factories in both New York and London. An eight horse-power steam engine could drive a ten cylinder Hoe machine to produce 25,000 impressions an hour.

Various media for stereotyping were used besides *papier mâché* in printing for purposes other than newspapers. Plaster of Paris and clay were common in flat-bed printing. For illustrations the production of plates by electrotyping was first used in 1840. Formerly illustrations for magazines and books had been produced from wooden blocks, from the surface of which an engraver had hollowed out all the parts which were to register as white in the finished picture, while all the parts which were to receive the ink and produce the black parts of the impression were left at the original level. The wooden blocks thus engraved would produce a certain number of excellent impressions when used with careful hand-printing. But the pressure introduced in steam-printing by machine soon crushed the projecting parts of the block and produced an

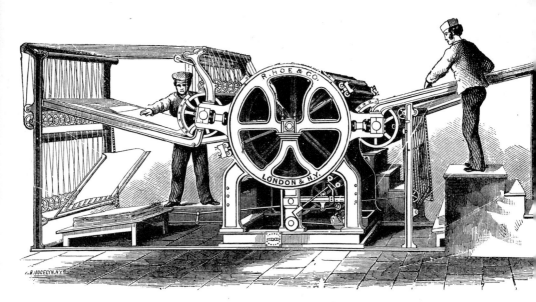

Hoe's Type Revolving Cylinder machine.

extremely muzzy illustration. The stereotype copy known as an electro-type was therefore used, leaving the original block as sharp as when first engraved and always available for a second electrotype if even that dur-able plate became worn. At first the mould for transfer to the plate was taken from the wood block on to gutta percha, a tough and flexible tropical gum. Later wax was adopted. The wax was melted and poured into a shallow pan where it was allowed to solidify. The surface was sprinkled with powdered blacklead. It was squeezed against the wood block in a very powerful press. The wax took on a very sharp and ex-tremely delicate and detailed impression while at the same time becom-ing very hard under the pressure. The face of the wax mould was again thoroughly blackleaded and the mould was suspended in a copper sul-phate solution with dilute sulphuric acid, and connected to a battery using copper wire as the positive electrode. By electro-deposition the blacklead received a deposit of copper which was about the thickness of a fingernail after about fifty hours' submersion. This thin shell of copper was then removed from the wax by the application of steam, which melted the wax away. The shell was then tinned on the back, and an alloy of lead with tin and antimony, forming the backing metal, was poured into the shell to the depth of about one eighth of an inch. When this had become solid the backing was planed so that the com-pound plate would have a certain regular thickness and the back surface was parallel to the face. The plate was trimmed and screwed down on to a wood block so that the face of the plate had the same height as any type that was to accompany it – either as a caption, title, or in-dependent copy on the same page or impression. The copper surface of this electrotype cast, with backing of the hard alloy, was considered the most durable surface that any printer could desire.

Lithography, that is, printing from drawings made on stone, was first encountered in England when a lithographic press was established in London in 1810 by a man called Hullmandel who had been tipped off about the new process, actually developed in Munich ten years earlier. Stones for lithography were prepared by being rubbed against each other, slab against slab, with a medium of sand and water. Stones in-tended to receive written characters were polished with pumice to an extra smoothness. Stones intended to receive drawings were given a sur-face with more grain by being uniformly rubbed with finely-sifted sand. When the design was to be applied to the stone, drawings were put on with lithographic crayon: a mixture of wax, soap, grease and lamp-black: Written characters, or the equivalent of pen-drawings, were put on with a special pen using lithographic ink, another specialised substance, a variation of the constituents of lithographic crayon, the essential ingredient being a waxy grease which would withstand the acid with which the stone was shortly to be treated. A lithographic artist worked in reverse characters of imposition straight on to the stone, but he had a mirror for seeing to check his work, and particularly his spelling. When the stone held the completed design a liquid containing nitric acid and gum was poured over it. The acid acted on all parts of the stone not protected by the ink or crayon. The stone so affected was in this manner made incapable of receiving printing ink. The stone was then well washed and cleaned with turpentine to remove the lithographic ink or crayon. Printer's ink was then applied by a roller, a sheet of damped paper was placed over the surface of the stone and the stone was passed with the paper under a roller to make the impression. Because stone, like wood, would eventually wear down with excessive printing from it, a number of transfers were made from the original on to fresh stones, according to the number calculated as required for the full publication. Up to 70,000 copies were taken from one drawing in this fashion.

Printing in colour by the method known as chromo-lithography was then developed as a means of reproducing works of art. The Victorian wonder of the chromo-lithograph was an extension of the publication of art by the availability of cheap reproductions that was entirely characteristic of the age. The skill in this craft was to print on the same paper with inks of different colours using a different stone for each colour applied. An individual stone was drawn only with that portion of the picture which was to receive the determined colour in the final product, and up to twenty stones were sometimes used for one reproduction. For cheaper and faster runs, such as magazine coloured supplements for gala occasions, colour-printing from a series of wooden blocks was employed. The final development, not perfected for popular reproduction by the late 1870s was the process of photo-lithography, which was intended to reproduce all the half-tones in a black-and-white photograph. For general journalism at this time most photographs were used as the basis for a fast engraving.

Increasingly in Victorian times the newspapers gathered their information swiftly by messages sent by the electric telegraph. This evolved from the discovery in 1819 of the intimate connection between electricity and magnetism. But even before this, attempts had been made to produce an electric telegraph working on what was then called Voltaic electricity – the phenomenon by which electrodes of zinc and copper placed in a bath of dilute acid can be made to decompose the water by producing bubbles of hydrogen if wires attached to the electrodes are connected. It was proposed that thirty-five pairs of electrodes should be arranged in a tank of dilute acid, each pair of electrodes marked to represent either a letter of the alphabet or one of the first nine numerals. Wires from these electrodes were to be connected to a distant transmitter, and when the correct connection for the letter A was made the electrodes marked A in the tank would produce their individual column of gas bubbles. This ingenious system was never adopted practically because of the number of wires required and a certain slowness and inaccuracy in determining where the bubbles were rising from. But with the discovery of electro-magnetism a number of schemes were conceived whereby a magnetic needle was subjected 'to differing charges of electricity at the transmitter – to which, as in all the 'electric telegraphs' utilised before the exploitation of wireless telegraphy, a continuous connection of wire between the transmitter and receiver was required – and the differing reactions of the needle could be interpreted in a code which would spell out the letters and numbers of messages. In 1837, the year of Victoria's accession, Charles Wheatstone (later Sir Charles) took out a patent for an electric telegraph in conjunction with Fothergill Cooke. Their machine had five magnetic needles arranged in a horizontal row, each needle being vertical when at rest but capable of being swung by electricity applied at the transmitter to various positions on the dial which were pre-marked with letters and numbers. This electric telegraph was immediately adopted by the London and Blackwall Railway. A year later Wheatstone and Cooke had reduced the number of needles to two, and eventually to one, and it was the economy resulting from the use of only one pair of wires, with the development that the transmitted message could be received at a number of sub-stations, that encouraged many of the railway companies, who then had most use for the system in signalling, to install the Wheatstone telegraph.

In 1845 there occurred a quite unconnected incident which dramatically emphasised the use of the electric telegraph in a manner exactly parallel to the means by which the murderer Crippen was arrested

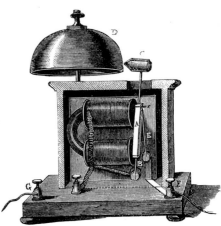

Electro-magnetic bells.

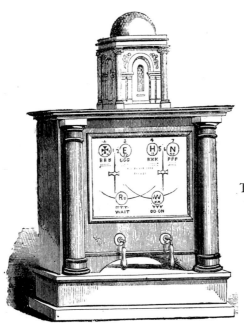

The Double-Needle Machine.

aboard the liner *Montrose* off the coast of Canada after a wireless message had been sent to the captain of the liner. The Crippen arrest, in 1911, is part of the folk-history of wireless telegraphy. The arrest of John Tawell after an electric telegraph message is now completely unknown, although at the time it was a public sensation of equivalent impact. A woman named Hart had been murdered at Salthill, near Eton. Tawell, the suspected murderer, had been traced to Slough station, where he had taken a train to London. A description of Tawell was telegraphed to London along with instructions to the police to tail the man after his arrival at Paddington. As a result of this telegraph message Tawell was followed, arrested, tried, convicted and executed. The incident was narrated with enthusiastic melodrama in a book by Sir Francis Head, a veteran soldier of Waterloo who, having been appointed Governor of Upper Canada in 1835, was such a failure that he provoked the armed rebellion two years later and was dismissed with a baronetcy, whereupon he took up the vocation of literary gentleman. He began his penny-dreadful with an analysis of the mind of the murderer, and finished with a deification of the electric telegraph as Nemesis the goddess of Revenge. An extract reads:

Whatever may have been his fears, his hopes, his fancies, or his thoughts, there suddenly flashed along the wires of the electric telegraph, which were stretched close beside him, the following words: 'A murder has just been committed at Salthill, and the suspected murderer was seen to take a first-class ticket to London by the train which left Slough at 7.42 p.m. He is in the garb of a Quaker, with a brown greatcoat on, which reaches nearly down to his feet. He is in the last compartment of the second first-class carriage.' And yet, fast as these words flew like lightning past him, the information they contained, with all its details, as well as every secret thought that had preceded them, had already consecutively flown millions of times faster; indeed, at the very instant that, within the walls of the little cottage at Slough, there had been uttered that dreadful scream, it had simultaneously reached the judgment-seat of Heaven! On arriving at the Paddington Station, after mingling for some moments with the crowd, he got into an omnibus, and as it rumbled along he probably felt that his identity was every minute becoming confounded and confused by the exchange of fellow-passengers for strangers that was constantly taking place. But all the time he was thinking, the cad [*i.e., conductor*] of the omnibus – a policeman in disguise – knew that he held his victim like a rat in a cage. Without, however, apparently taking the slightest notice of him, he took one sixpence, gave change for a shilling, handed out this lady, stuffed in that one, until, arriving at the Bank, the guilty man, stooping as he walked towards the carriage door, descended the steps, paid his fare, crossed over to the Duke of Wellington's statue, where, pausing for a few moments, anxiously to gaze around him, he proceeded to the Jerusalem Coffee-house, thence over London Bridge to the Leopard Coffee-house in the Borough, and, finally, to a lodging-house in Scott's Yard, Cannon Street. He probably fancied that, by making so many turns and doubles, he had not only effectually puzzled all pursuit, but that his appearance at so many coffee-houses would assist him, if necessary, in proving an *alibi*; but, whatever may have been his motives or his thoughts, he had scarcely entered the lodging when the policeman – who, like a wolf, had followed him every step of the way – opening his door, very calmly said to him – the words, no doubt, were infinitely more appalling to him even than the scream which had been haunting him – 'Haven't you just come from Slough?' The monosyllable, 'No,' confusedly uttered in reply, substantiated his guilt. The policeman made him his prisoner; he was thrown into jail, tried, found guilty of wilful murder, and hanged. A few months afterwards we happened to be travelling by rail from Paddington to Slough, in a carriage filled with people all strangers to one another. Like English travellers, they were mute. For nearly fifteen miles no one had uttered a single word, until a short-bodied, short-necked, short-nosed, exceedingly respectable-looking man in the corner, fixing his eyes on the apparently fleeting posts and rails of the electric telegraph, significantly nodded to us as he muttered aloud, 'Them's the cords that hung John Tawell!'

Wheatstone and Cooke were the pioneers of the practical use of the electric telegraph but they were not the only men in the field. Samuel Morse had been working on the idea since 1832, and he invented (with Alfred Vail) the Morse Code in 1837, the year in which Wheatstone and Cooke's electric telegraph was patented and adopted. The reason why the Morse system overhauled Wheatstone and may be said to have triumphed in the end was that Morse from the start was concerned with sending messages by the electric telegraph which were self-recording. Wheatstone's self-recording system was adopted widely in England but was eventually supplanted by Morse. Samuel Morse was a 41-year-old artist who had studied in England, returned to his American home to become president of the National Academy of Design in New York, but had also taken an interest in chemistry and electricity, when he first applied himself seriously to the principle of the electric telegraph. On a voyage from Cherbourg to New York aboard the steamer *Sully* in

[84]

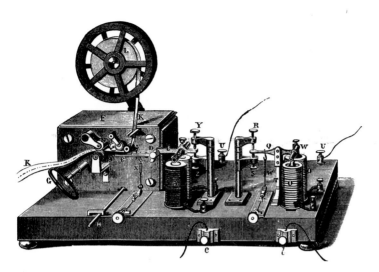

The Morse Recording Telegraph.

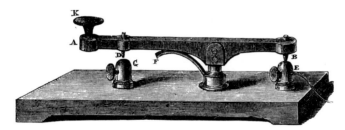

A Morse Transmitting Key.

October 1832 he had mentioned the subject to a fellow-voyager, an American professor named Jackson. Jackson was at the time more of an expert on electricity than Morse, and he advanced certain ideas by which electric telegraphy might be accomplished. These were apparently impractical, but when later Morse developed his system and began to make money with it Jackson claimed that he had had a substantial responsibility for the invention, and began a famous law-suit against Morse which he eventually lost. Morse developed his system, of which the electro-magnetic recorder was an integral part, abandoned the profession of art altogether, and saw a minor utilisation of his telegraph adopted in America in 1837. It was not however until 1844, when a telegraph line authorised by Congress at the cost of $30,000 connected Baltimore and Washington and used the Morse system, that he could have been said to have broken through the conservative opposition against him. His success was however far more spectacular than Wheatstone's, which was confined to the British Isles, for in a short space of time seven Governments in Europe, and Turkey in addition, had adopted the Morse system and apparatus, and he was notching an immediate financial success. Wheatstone had in the meantime ingeniously improved the system whereby a dial holding all the letters and and numbers could be operated by a person at one end of the line and would reproduce with a needle the same deflections to the letters and numbers at the other end of the line, and this method, after further refinements, was commonly used in commercial life and by some state institutions in Europe because of its advantage of not requiring a highly trained telegraphist with a knowledge of morse to operate it.

A century ago, therefore, there were four systems in use exploiting the electric telegraph. The first was the method by which current was made to deflect magnetised needles. In the second the current magnetised soft iron and caused an indicator to swing across a dial and point to the letter or numeral which had been signalled. In the third a current working on soft iron printed the messages, either in ordinary type or in a code. The fourth operated by emitting sound only. Where alphabetic letters and simple numerals were indicated and recorded, less operator training was necessary but the apparatus was more complicated and more likely to break down. Where code was used the preliminary training was more intense but the apparatus was simpler and more reliable. Although nowadays everyone can recognise the sound of morse, even if they cannot read it, if only because we have grown up with radio and film sound effects, morse was not at first read by the sound of it, which was merely an incidental to the recording of it on paper. The first electric telegraph based on sound alone was the instrument adopted by the United States War Department in which the signals were conveyed, not by the deflection of a needle, but by blows of an electro-magnet on its armature – the make-and-break blows, in fact, which are made by any electric bell. The American Army telegraph used only two basic symbols: a single stroke and a rapid double stroke, known always as a One and a Two. The alphabet used was the General Service Flag Code of the American Army and Navy, and the Ones and the Twos were transmitted by a key very similar to that used in morse. The Flag Code took very slightly longer to transmit than the morse code: B, for instance was 2112 as against dash-dot-dot-dot in the morse code, and F 2221 as against dot-dot-dash-dot. But there were never more than four elements in the signal for a letter, as indeed was the case with the morse code, though an additional symbol was required for numerals and two extra for punctuation marks. The American Service telegrams were, however, only read by the sound. There was no record of what had been sent beyond the transmitter's copy and the receiver's version, and there was always the possibility of human error intervening. With unrecorded transmissions the messages could not be read at leisure except by a record sheet made simultaneously by hand, which was not then the practice in military operations, and errors which might have occurred in transmission could not be traced to their source. A system which registered the messages as actually received had plainly many advantages over those which merely gave a visible or audible signal without leaving any trace. It was this disadvantage which Samuel Morse strove from the beginning to surmount. His aim was to achieve the indelible recording of telegraphed messages, and it was only by the quick skill of the operators that morse began to be 'read' from the sound: it was a sort of trick that operators acquired. Nowadays in military circles and in the mercantile marine the instant reading of morse is the first requirement. It is only in world communications as conducted by the Post Office and the commercial cable and radio companies, where a mechanical speeding-up of transmission has pushed the reception of messages to a velocity which the ear cannot master, that the original principle has been revived that morse is to be recorded and afterwards 'translated' – though nowadays both

[87]

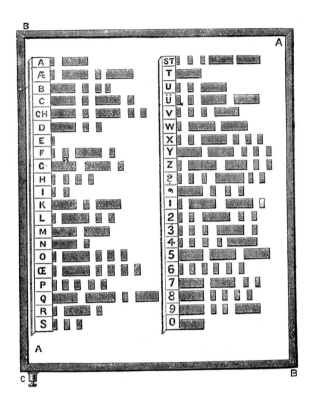

The Morse Transmitting Plate

transmission and translation are effected at a speed which only mechanical means can achieve.

The original Morse recording telegraph received the signals from the transmitter in a combination of short and long impulses which we now call dots and dashes. When the operator at the transmitter depressed his key long enough to transmit a dash the current was switched on long enough in the receiver to work an electro-magnet which attracted one end of a hinged lever for the length of time we now accept as a dash. At the other end of the lever was a blunt steel point, and as long as the current was on, that point was pushed up into a shallow groove on a metal roller around which a paper ribbon was being unwound by clockwork. As soon as the current transmitting the dash ceased, the other end of the lever was not attracted to move by magnetism, and the end of the lever with the steel point was removed from the paper. If a dot was transmitted the duration of the current impulse would be less and the steel embossing the message would be in contact with the paper ribbon for a shorter time. This was the original recording telegraph. It was improved when it was provided with mechanism to print the symbols in ink from a constantly-charged roller, instead of embossing the code, a procedure which demanded far less force of current to activate the lever. The variations of dot and dash as symbols for the letters and numerals had been worked out by Morse so that the letters most frequently recurring in the English language were given the shortest symbols. The letter E, as the most frequent letter used, was given a single dot. The letter T, which Morse thought was the next most frequently used, was given a single dash. The letters A (dot-dash), I (dot-dot), M (dash-dash) and N (dash-dot) were next allocated with the most economical transmission symbols. But it is interesting that the American Edgar Allan Poe, who was writing that classic of decipherment *The Gold Bug* at about the same time as Morse was devising his code, differed widely from Morse in his account of the frequency of the letters in the English language. He gave, in fact, a precise run-down of frequency: 'Now, in English, the letter which most frequently occurs is E. Afterwards the succession runs thus: A O I D H N R S T U Y C F G L M W B K P Q X Z.' But Poe may have been writing very fast at the time, since he missed out the letters J and V – which admittedly were sometimes in older calligraphy taken to be the same as I and U.

A development of Morse's recording telegraph was the provision of a

[89]

relay. This was intended to boost the current from a distant transmitter which, on reception, might not be powerful enough to magnetise the soft iron in the receiver with sufficient intensity to give clear signals. In effect the current received called on the power of a local battery at the instant the distant signal was received, and energised the punch or recording pen sufficiently to make unmistakable impressions. Sir Charles Wheatstone eventually accepted the morse code when the Post Office within Great Britain took over all public telegraphic transmission, but he slightly adapted the recording of it to attain greater speed, in effect by cutting out the dashes and recording them at a different level in his paper ribbon, but using dots instead of dashes. In introducing this system in a machine which at the time greatly increased the speed of the process, Wheatstone defined his three sets of apparatus:

Long strips of paper are perforated by a machine constructed for the purpose, with apertures grouped to represent the letters of the alphabet and other signs. A strip thus prepared is placed in an instrument associated with a source of electric power, which, on being set in motion, moves it along, and causes it to act on two pins in such a manner that when one of them is elevated the current is transmitted to the telegraphic circuit in one direction, when the other is elevated the current is transmitted in the reverse direction. The elevations and depressions of these pins are governed by the apertures and intervening intervals. These currents, following each other indifferently in these two opposite directions, act upon a writing instrument at a distant station in such a manner as to produce corresponding marks on a slip of paper, moved by appropriate mechanism. The first apparatus is a *perforator*, an instrument for piercing the slips of paper with the apertures in the order required to form the message. The slip of paper passes through a guiding groove, at the bottom of which an opening is made sufficiently large to admit of the to-and-fro motion of the upper end of a frame containing three punches, the extremities of which are in the same transverse line. Each of these punches, the middle one of which is smaller than the two external ones, may be separately elevated by the pressure of a finger-key. By the pressure of either finger-key, simultaneously with the elevation of its corresponding punch, in order to perforate the paper, two different movements are successively produced: first, the raising of a clip which holds the paper firmly in its position; and secondly, the advancing motion of the frame containing the three punches, by which the punch which is raised carries the slip of paper forward the proper distance. During the reaction of the key consequent on the removal of the pressure, the clip first fastens the paper, and then the frame falls back to its normal position. The two external keys and punches are employed to make the holes, which, grouped together, represent letters and other characters, and the middle punch to make holes which mark the intervals between the letters. The second apparatus is the *transmitter*, the object of which is to receive the slips of paper prepared by the perforator, and to transmit the currents in the order and direction corresponding to the holes perforated in the slip. This it effects by mechanism somewhat similar to that by which the perforator performs its functions. An eccentric produces and regulates the occurrence of three distinct movements: 1, the to-and-fro motion of a small frame which contains a groove fitted to receive the slip of paper, and to carry it forward by its advancing motion. 2, the elevation and depression of a spring-clip, which holds the slip of paper firmly during the receding motion, but allows it to move freely during the advancing motion. 3, the simultaneous elevation of three wires placed parallel to each other, resting at one of their ends over the axis of the eccentric, and their free ends entering corresponding holes in the grooved frame. These three wires are not fixed to the axis of the eccentric, but each end of them rests against it by the upward pressure of a spring; so that when a light pressure is exerted on the free end of either of them, it is capable of being separately depressed. When the slip of paper is not inserted the eccentric is in action; a pin attached to each of the external wires touches during the advancing and receding motions of the frame a different spring; and an arrangement is adopted, by means of insulation and contacts properly applied, by which, while one of the wires is elevated, the other remains depressed; the current passes to the telegraphic circuit in one direction, and passes in the other direction when the wire before elevated is depressed, and vice versa; but while both wires are simultaneously elevated or depressed the passing of the current is interrupted. When the prepared slip of paper is inserted in the groove, and moved forward whenever one of the wires enters an aperture in its corresponding row, the current passes in one direction, and when the end of the other wire enters an aperture of the other row, it passes in the other direction. By this means the currents are made to succeed each other *automatically* in their proper order and direction to give the requisite variety of signals. The middle wire only acts as a guide during the operation of the current. The wheel which drives the eccentric may be moved by hand or by the application of any motive power. Where the movement of the transmitter is effected by machinery, any number may be attended to by one or two assistants. This transmitter requires only a single telegraphic wire. The third apparatus is the *recording* or *printing apparatus*, which prints or impresses legible marks on a strip of paper, corresponding in their arrangement with the apertures on the perforated paper. The pens or styles are elevated or depressed by their connection with the moving parts of

[91]

electro-magnets. The pens are entirely independent of each other in their action, and are so arranged that when the current passes through the coils of the electro-magnet in one direction, one of the pens is depressed, and when it passes in the contrary direction the other is depressed; when the currents cease, light springs release and restore the pens to their elevated points. The mode of supplying the pens with ink is as follows: A reservoir about an eighth of an inch deep, and of any convenient length and breadth, is made in a piece of metal, the interior of which may be gilt in order to avoid the corrosive action of the ink; at the bottom of this reservoir are two holes, sufficiently small to prevent by capillary attraction the ink from flowing through them; the ends of the pens are placed immediately above these small apertures, which they enter when the electro-magnets act upon them, carrying with them a sufficient charge of ink to make a legible mark on a ribbon of paper passing beneath them. The motion of the paper ribbon is produced and regulated by apparatus similar to those employed in other register and printing telegraphs.

This invention of Wheatstone, patented in 1862 and put fully into perfected action in 1867, was wonder enough at the time. The most astonishing fact is that a century later it was still in use on submarine cables because of its superiority in speed over teleprinter working, being capable of working at 300 words a minute. The only modern development has been a re-perforator which is used to produce a perforated tape at the receiving end precisely similar to that at the transmitting end. This tape may be used to re-transmit the message by passing it through an automatic transmitter connected to another circuit, or by passing it through a specially designed printing instrument which records the message in normal characters.

The teleprinter which has been mentioned as inferior in speed to the Wheatstone recording apparatus actually existed a century ago though it had not been given that name. An inventor called Hughes produced a recording telegraph in which the message was printed at the receiving station in orthodox Roman characters. Since only a single instantaneous current needed to be sent for each letter, the speed with which a message could be sent was even at that time three times as great as was available from the Morse instrument. These advantages were obtained then, however, only at the cost of great delicacy and complexity in the apparatus. Not only highly skilled operators were required, but also a corps of specialist mechanics and electricians to correct the faults which developed. There were other forms of print-out telegraph recorders, most of

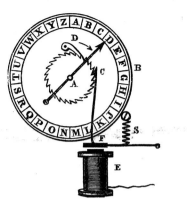

The Step-by-step movement.

Froment's Dials.

them based on the principle of the dial telegraph, in which on a sort of clock face the 26 letters of the alphabet and the ten basic numerals were marked. A ratchet wheel containing 36 teeth to correspond with the characters on the dial was mounted on a central axis. One momentary burst of current was released every time the dial was swung past one character, so that if the operator advanced his dial by six spaces to rest on the letter F, a similar progression was made on the dial at the receiving end. A further telegraphic invention was the facsimile copying telegraph, which sent messages automatically after they had been set up in type. The copying at the receiver was done on a kind of photographic paper which needed developing, but the action was very fast and it was claimed that 1200 words could be sent and received between stations hundreds of miles apart within a minute.

Overhead land lines for telegraphy were constructed a century ago from iron wire of about one-sixth of an inch diameter, coated with zinc or 'galvanised' in the same way as the old-fashioned galvanised zinc baths. (The Victorians used the word 'galvanise' or 'galvanic' in three senses, all concerned with electricity: a galvanic pile was a primary battery; to galvanise was to stimulate, as if by electricity, as well as to coat with metal by electrolysis – the root of all the words was the name of the Italian Luigi Galvani, a professor of anatomy at Bologna who published his 'discovery' of electricity in animal muscle in 1791.) In urban districts where the air contained sulphur or noxious acids carried in industrial smoke the lines were tarred or varnished to combat corrosion. Underground lines were made of copper encased in gutta-percha and laid in wooden troughs or iron pipes. Submarine cables were developed early as the result of independent experiments conducted by Morse and Wheatstone at exactly the same time, in 1843. They became practical possibilities when the insulating properties of gutta-percha were established, and the first international cable under the sea was laid between Dover and Cap Gris Nez in the late 1840s. Unfortunately it lasted only long enough to prove that its electrical properties worked, but not its metallic strength, for within a week it was cut by the action of the sharp rocks near the French coast on which it lay. After further experiment a cable was devised consisting of four insulated copper wires spun with tarred hemp to make a rope and then given an outer casing of thick iron wire wound spirally on it, ten strands at a time. This cable, weighing seven tons to the mile and 27 miles long, was successfully laid in 1851 and continued in use through the century, though there were occasional breakages which had to be repaired. This cable was immediately imitated in others laid from Great Britain to Holland, Ireland and Germany. The success of these enterprises encouraged the laying of a transatlantic cable. With the astonishing speed which the Victorians displayed in this sort of endeavour, a cable was devised to meet the specifications and a speculative public subscribed over a quarter of a million pounds to get in on the ground floor of the enterprise. The first cable had been laid to a distance of 338 miles when, in 1857, the line parted and the cable – already weighing some 3400 tons – was lost. The engineers set themselves to devising cable with a higher breaking-strain along with improved paying-out apparatus and self-releasing brakes for the drums aboard the cable-laying ships. The laying of the next cable began in mid-ocean, with two cable-laying ships gradually retreating from each other as they paid the line out. The cable parted three times, and the ships had to steam back to meet each other, repair the severed cable and start laying all over again. On 5 August 1858 a true cable connection between Britain and the United States was effected: but after only a month an electrical fault developed and the continuity was cut. By 1865 the *Great Eastern* had been converted as a cable-laying ship, and a cable of a greatly improved design was manufactured. It contained seven copper wires twisted into one strand and covered first with several layers of insulation and externally with woven tarred hemp. This cable was altogether 2600 miles long, and it contained 25,000 miles of copper wire, an even greater length of iron wire, and some 400,000 miles of hemp rope. It was loaded aboard the *Great Eastern* in sections of 800 miles contained in gigantic iron tanks each with a laden weight of 5800 tons. The ship paid out 1186 miles of cable over a steaming distance of 1062 miles from Valentia, the shore base, when the electricians aboard the *Great Eastern* discerned a loss of insulation. The ship had to steam back, picking up the cable and examining every foot before passing it back to the bottom of the sea. In the course of this operation the cable parted. It was at a point where the Atlantic was believed to be a mile deep. The broken cable was picked up by grapnels, and it continually broke from strain during the lifting operation. The *Great Eastern* had to return to base with cable that had cost a million and a quarter pounds lying uselessly at the bottom of the sea. The engineers and the commercial promoters, supported by the British investing public, did not lose

Wires being made for the Atlantic Telegraph Cable.

heart but determined to try again. Within three years another cable had been manufactured, and this time the *Great Eastern* made an astonishingly smooth and fast trip, arriving at Newfoundland in fifteen days for the cable to be spliced to the shore section there on 28 July 1868. The *Great Eastern* then steamed back to retrieve the lost cable of 1865, located it by buoys that had been set as markers, picked it up, repaired it, found its electrical condition unharmed after the original insulation fault had been corrected, spliced on a new cable and made for Newfoundland again, to complete the laying of the second transatlantic cable. The establishment of this literally instantaneous communication between the two continents allowed an unprecedented surge in the commerce between east and west. It also revolutionised the transmission and publication of news. The mails had previously taken a fortnight to arrive. Now a political speech in London could be printed in New York in full detail apparently even before it had been delivered, according to the confusing time-scale based on the difference in longitude. The telegraph was of course also used extensively for private messages, personal and romantic, in an age when a quite extraordinary number of English gentlemen were setting off to the American prairie for hunting expeditions enlivened by the opportunities to sow a few wild oats in the establishments provided for frustrated bachelors in the frontier towns. Many a Victorian miss sent cautionary reminders to her man to remind him that he was no longer out of touch or beyond supervision. Marriages were arranged, and sometimes broken off, by submarine cable. If the laws of England could have been slightly bent to match the American model, marriages could even have been celebrated by this means. This was certainly the case inside the United States. Just over a century ago there occurred one of the first 'crazy' American marriages, a precursor of the hundreds that have occurred since between practising pole-squatters, marathon dancers, deep-water divers, and circus artists getting spliced while bareback riding. A Boston merchant was putting pressure on his daughter to marry a man for whom she had no affection at all. The object of her affections was a young gallant who had left the city to go to England but had so far only reached New York. She determined that she had better marry Mr Right as speedily as possible. She made a complicated series of arrangements by telegraph. At an agreed time after all the instructions had been given, she attended a telegraph office in Boston with a judge in her party. The young man was at the same time

[97]

in a telegraph office in New York with another judge. With a copy of the morse code in the left hand and the marriage service on the desk in front of them, they struggled with the morse key to exchange their vows, and they were duly pronounced as married by telegraph. The father tried to contest the marriage, but after taking legal advice he decided that he could not annul the proceedings. The couple had clicked, and he was powerless as a circuit-breaker.

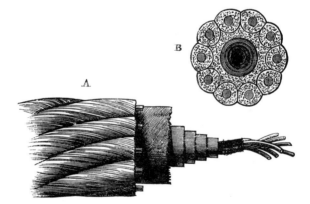

The Atlantic Telegraph Cable, 1866.

SIX
THE SAFETY OF LIFE

THE Royal National Lifeboat Institution was founded in Britain, forty years ahead of any similar service in any other country, in 1824 as the National Institution for the Preservation of Life from Shipwreck, and since that time it has continued to save lives at the astonishing rate of twelve a week, or well over 60,000 a century. But since the beginning of the nineteenth century there had been 45 mortar stations around the coast, theoretically capable of firing projectiles to take a rescue line over a wrecked ship, and greatly improved in their performance when rockets of great power had been developed. From the beginning of the century also a theoretically unsinkable lifeboat had been available for building according to the design of William Wouldhave, but it was not until the South Shields lifeboat capsized at the mouth of the Tyne in 1849, drowning twenty of her crew, that the self-righting lifeboat, with high air chambers fore and aft and a disproportionately heavy keel, was generally recommended. The trouble with this design was that it was more likely to capsize, because of the height of its end sections, than a boat of conventional design, although it would undoubtedly right itself once it had deposited its crew in the water. But in the matter of the safety of life at sea, the most marked feature of nineteenth century progress was in the improvement of lighthouses in both structure and illumination. Even the famous Eddystone lighthouse, which had been a triumph òf construction by Smeaton, burned tallow candles stuck in a hoop until 1799, when it was converted to an oil-fired light. A century ago the use of electricity was being only gradually introduced in lighthouses where the conditions were favourable. One of the most difficult tasks of lighthouse building in that era was the construction of the light on the Skerryvore Reef, twelve miles from Tyree, the island now so familiar as a name in the broadcast weather information for shipping which is situated off the coast of Argyllshire. It is considerably higher and broader-based than the Eddystone, with a height of 138 feet and a base diameter of 42 feet, and this mass was considered necessary because it is one of the few lighthouses where the stones on the outer face are not dove-tailed or joggled, a form of binding which was and is usually considered necessary for any lighthouse constantly exposed to the open sea. Its engineer, Alan Stevenson, found that the rocks were of gneiss, a very hard and coarsely-banded crystalline rock which in fact gave its name to the Hebrides, when they were called the Gneiss Islands. Stevenson found that the rocks of Skerryvore Reef had surfaces worn as smooth as glass by the action of the water. He chose to build his lighthouse on a very narrow strip of rock which was the only part of the reef which projected above high water, although at low tide the area was strewn with the series of rising islands which indicated the reef. But because of the existence of these other rocks, though they were invisible at high water, the sea rushed tumultuously in dangerously fast-flowing gullies which created a turbulence which significantly threatened the structure. Stevenson began work in 1838 by sinking piles at a spot conveniently near the proposed site of the lighthouse and erecting a wooden building on the top of the piles. But during a winter gale the whole of this structure was swept away in a single night. Stevenson had to wait until summer before he could build a replacement which had to be greatly reinforced. In this semi-shelter he and his men would sometimes be marooned for a fortnight at a time when the state of the sea prevented their going ashore. Sometimes at dead of night the men were roused by the waves pouring over the roof of the building and forcing their way inside through every crevice. There were times when they feared so forcibly that the whole structure would be washed away that they abandoned it and spent the night clinging to the rocks, to which they had shackled themselves, preferring to choke in the seas breaking over their bodies rather than risk being carried away with not even a hand-grip on the rocks. The work of cutting the rock for the foundations took two summers, and the space available was so confined that every blasting operation presented moments of considerable danger. Part of their work was to cut a small harbour in the reef for the shelter of the ships bringing the prepared stones for the lighthouse from the shore, where they were briefly moored to specially made piers. Stevenson had determined to rely on massive weight to keep his structure stable rather than the usual dove-tailing or joggle-jointing of the stones. He measured the force of the waves at Skerryvore as approaching a maximum pressure of 4335 pounds per square foot, and worked out the weight of superstructure that would be necessary to withstand this force. For this reason he decided on the broad base, and eventually he put 59,000 cubic feet of stone into the Skerryvore light, a volume which was about five times the bulk of the Eddystone, built in 1759. The total cost of the new building was £87,000.

The Skerryvore went into operation in 1844, and by the expert enthusiasm of Alan Stevenson it was the first British lighthouse to be fitted with catadioptric apparatus for the illumination. There are three artificial aids for achieving a concentration of the light issued from a lighthouse tower. The first is by reflection from mirrors and is effected by what is called catoptric apparatus. The second is by refraction through lenses, a method which was introduced early in the nineteenth century, and through Stevenson's energetic recommendation was first adopted in Great Britain in 1835. It is done by what is called the dioptric method. The development of this sytem, which speedily super-seded the others, is a combination of the two previous methods, so that light-rays are first refracted and then reflected in the system called catadioptric. In the Skerryvore the light was refracted almost at source, at what is called the incident face. The rays were then totally reflected by mirrors at a second face, and then were again refracted as they emerged at the third face. Before the nineteenth century, when only burning wood or coal or occasionally candles were used for the source of light, there was little concentration possible. Occasionally sheets of brass were placed behind the light to reflect the glow out to sea. When the source of light became stronger a parabolic mirror was introduced – the mirror which reflected all light falling on it as a cylindrical beam parallel to the axis of the mirror. At the beginning of the century these were made of sheet copper thickly plated with silver to an extent of coating the copper with $37\frac{1}{2}$ per cent of its weight of silver. The copper had been shaped by beating circular sheets into a concave shape which was finally brought by gauges to the exact shape, after which it was turned and polished. These reflectors could be up to two feet in diameter

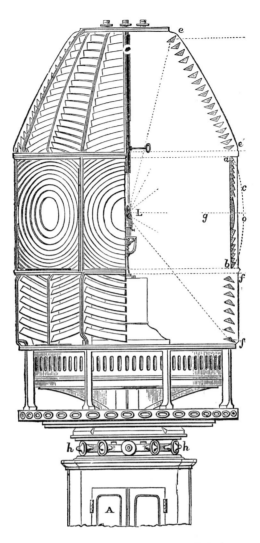

Section of a revolving light in a lighthouse.

at the mouth, which meant that the beam cast from the curve would be a cylinder of two feet diameter. A greater number of beams would be cast by increasing the number of parabolic mirrors, in the intervals around the circumference of the lantern which had been decided on to convey the identity of the particular lighthouse. The frame of mirrors was rotated by clockwork at a fixed speed and thus swept the sky on all sides. In areas of coast where the dangers were numerous and the number of lighthouses had to be multiplied, so that more than one could be visible at one time, the identity was given either by further combinations of colour – with a red beam, for example, as part of the succession of whites – or by flashing lights in which the intensity of the beam increased and decreased at regular intervals, or by intermittent lights where a screen on the revolving frame cut off the light for part of the revolution. Because of the situation and atmospheric conditions of lighthouses it was found that the reflectors became increasingly inefficient because of the speedy loss of polish on the surfaces which reduced their carrying power by as much as one half. The English were the first to attempt to master the problem by substituting glass lenses for polished reflectors, but at that time refraction produced a less powerful beam. The Frenchman Fresnel perceived that refraction would give a more intense beam only if the focal length of the lens could be made very short and the diameter very great. But the dimensions necessary would call for very thick glass, which would both diminish the volume of light issuing and impose an intolerable weight on the revolving frame – and in any case no lighthouse then built could accept the size of lens required. He hit upon the idea of constructing the *lentille à échelons*, or stepped lens. Basically he built a series of concentric lenses, each of which had the same focal length. By this construction of a series of different lenses in one frame he was able to cut away the thickness of the glass which would have been required for one lens producing the same effect. In addition he placed vertically above and below the circumference of the composite lens a series of prisms which by refraction and total reflections sent the rays of light which they caught out on the same path as the light refracted by the lens, that is, parallel to the axis of the lens. Fresnel then set himself to develop a much more intense light in order fully to exploit the lens he had developed. As commissioner of lighthouses for the French Government, Augustin Fresnel was using the lamp invented by the

[103]

Swiss chemist Aimé Argand which was known as the Argand Burner. This had been a revolutionary improvement when it was adopted, but it now needed improvement. The Argand Burner was an oil lamp with a tubular wick which introduced a current of air through the hollow of the metal tubes enclosing the wick, and the air, rising within the frame, achieved more oxidation and a brighter light, especially when combined with the new shape of glass lamp chimney, pinched in at the top of the flame, which is now the conventional shape for all oil lamp chimneys. Having, by the introduction of air, achieved the complete burning of the oil offered to the wick, with a brighter light resulting, the next step was to increase the supply of oil. Argand had relied on ordinary capillary action to keep the oil moving into the wick. The Frenchman Carcel had increased the flow of oil by a clockwork pump which continually pumped up the oil into the burner, so that, by overflowing, the oil was maintained at an invariable level with a consequent improvement in the intensity and steadiness of the light. Fresnel now set out to increase the number of wicks in order to generate more light. Working with Dominique Arago, a French physicist and astronomer who was his colleague in the far more theoretical development of the wave theory of light, Fresnel developed a lamp with several concentric wicks which ultimately produced a light 25 times more brilliant than that obtained from a single-wick Argand lamp, though it did not quite demand 25 times the amount of oil. The oil originally used in lighthouse lamps was sperm oil, but for this they had substituted colza, or rape oil, obtained from the seeds of a brassica mainly grown in the East. By 1837 coal gas had been introduced for those lighthouses where a supply was available, and in specialised burners it gave a light of improved brilliance and steadiness. Petroleum oil was tried, but at that time could be used only with one burner wick. Electric light, at first using arc-lamps, was brought in 1858 and was installed in the South Foreland lighthouse in 1862. But as far as the optical apparatus was concerned, the Skerryvore light built by Alan Stevenson contained every feature that was maintained in the most advanced lighthouses for many years to come. The height of the light chamber, that is, the accommodation for the lenses and prisms around the central lamp, was almost nine feet and the lantern measured over six feet in diameter. The lantern was octagonal, with eight Fresnel composite lenses arranged around its circumference, each lens being roughly 28 inches in diameter.

Above each lens there were two vertical rows of 18 reflecting prisms, and below each lens two rows of eight reflecting prisms. The whole lantern was encased in an outer metal framework glazed with thick plate glass. The height of the Skerryvore, at 138 feet, neared the optimum height for lighthouses, which would be impractical at a a much greater distance. In isolated lighthouses such as Skerryvore a path into the sky because of the curvature of the earth. A light displayed one hundred feet above the water can be seen from the deck of a ship fourteen miles away, and from the masthead could be seen at a much greater distance. In isolated lighthouses such as Skerryvore a staff of four keepers was normal, with allowance for one of the keepers always to be absent on shore leave. The custom of having three keepers on duty, with two of them splitting up the darkness watch, was adopted after a grim incident earlier in the nineteenth century at the lighthouse on the Smalls Rock in the Bristol Channel. That lighthouse was then staffed by two men. At one time it could not be relieved for four months owing to continuous stormy weather. But after the lighthouse had been cut off for two weeks look-outs on passing ships had seen a distress signal. The ships, however, could not get within speaking distance of the lighthouse because of the weather. The news of some distress naturally became known on shore, and the families of the two keepers became anxious. Nightly they looked out, but never once did they fail to see the light come on at the proper time. Finally calm weather intervened and a boat was sent out to relieve the lighthouse crew. They brought back one dead and the other alive. One man had found his companion dead when he awoke and went on duty. He decided that he could not bury his crew-mate at sea because suspicion might arise that he had killed him. He therefore dragged the corpse up to the gallery of the lighthouse, built a rough coffin and took that up too, and put the corpse in the coffin and lashed the coffin to the gallery. For the rest of that four-months spell of duty he performed all the work alone, staying up in the light-chamber, with his dead friend outside, from twilight until dawn and then setting about his essential tasks of cleaning the glass, adjusting and oiling the machinery, keeping the light supplied with fuel and the wicks trimmed. He never got over the effect that the ordeal had had on him, and from the moment he stepped ashore he was an entirely changed man.

The saving of life by the avoidance of fatal shock during surgical operations and an over-stoical endurance of childbirth – which, apart from the considerations of its intolerable frequency and great risk of infection, sent many a Victorian mother early to the grave – was overcome in this period of nineteenth century history by the acceptance of anaesthetics. Sir Humphry Davy had actually published work on anaesthesia in 1800, but the practical implications of his work were largely ignored for nearly half a century. When the use of anaesthetics was finally adopted the new prospects of survival and of the extinction of pain were hailed as an almost miraculous Victorian wonder, amid fervent declarations that in the entire annals of the healing art no other modern discovery had so largely and so directly contributed to the assuagement of human suffering. Davy, when he was only 21, published *Researches, Chemical and Philosophical, chiefly concerning Nitrous Oxide and its Respiration.* His work caused such a sensation that, although he had qualified as a doctor, he was persuaded to follow his other enthusiasm of chemistry and took up a number of academic posts which led to his becoming Professor of Chemistry at the Royal Institution. Davy had not discovered nitrous oxide, but he was the first to make a full investigation into its nature and properties, and he certainly had the researcher's courage to try the administration of the laughing gas on himself: he had a tooth painlessly extracted while under its influence. Therefore, in his publication of 1800 he suggested that, as nitrous oxide had the property of cancelling pain it could quite feasibly be used 'in surgical operations where there is no effusion of blood'. Although surgeons did not publicly adopt this anaesthesia even as an experiment, the properties of the gas were not only well known, but consistently demonstrated to students in medical schools. The embryo doctors were persuaded to take individual sniffs of the gas and, although no surgery was attempted on them, they were jovially pinched and punched while unconscious as a demonstration to the jaunty Sawbones that they had no memory or any recollection of pain endured at the time when their soreness was inflicted. In 1818, when these pranks were a byword in the hospitals, Michael Faraday, the young chemist, philosopher and pioneer of electrical theory, who after attending some of Humphry Davy's lectures had prevailed on him to take him on as an assistant, pointed out the similarity between the effects of ether, a derivative of alcohol, and the consequences of taking nitrous oxide. From that time Professor Turner, an academic chemistry tutor in London, regularly added a dose of ether to the practical experiments which he induced his students to carry out – simply passing his selected victim a wad impregnated with ether and asking him to smell it. These hilarious demonstrations went on for another 26 years, by which time a whole new generation of doctors had grown up with an awareness of the knock-out drops though they had done nothing about it, and the comic exhibitions had now been adopted by public lecturers who were agreeable to the display, for money received, of the marvels of modern chemistry. These lectures were highly popular in the United States also. In 1844 a dentist in Hartford, Connecticut, named Horace Wells attended one of these lectures and saw the process of the application of nitrous oxide to a volunteer. Horace had an appointment next morning with another dentist, for he had diagnosed that he himself needed a tooth extracted. Knowing something of the pain he was regularly causing to others, and feeling unable to endure it himself, he went to the stage door after the lecture and prevailed on the lecturer to come to his surgery next morning and administer the nitrous oxide before his brother surgeon got to work. The lecturer agreed, and acted as anaesthetist for a consideration. Horace Wells came laughing out of his temporary dream, with a hole in his gum but no misery preceding it, and exclaimed 'A new era in tooth-pulling!' He applied himself to learning the technique of the use of nitrous oxide, but his tuition was inefficient, his results were sometimes scarifying, and because of the variations in the effect on his patients he abandoned the technique. He had, however, invited Dr W. T. G. Morton to be present at his original self-inflicted wound, and Morton, with more persistence, had gone on to experiment with both nitrous oxide and ether vapour, and had found that not only tooth extraction but quite drastic surgical operations could be performed under their influence without the serious shock of pain. Morton tried to make a fortune from his discovery, which he was entitled to do, but he used the wrong technique. He obtained a patent for a substance inducing forgetfulness which he named Letheon. But ether has a highly characteristic smell, and Morton had omitted in his innocence to mix a harmless essence like oil of cloves with it for purposes of disguise. Consequently, when a rival doctor named Bigelow bought a bottle of Letheon and recognised the smell, he went straight to the manufacturing chemists to order ether. He then applied it in his medical practice after various experiments, using it for the comparatively

[107]

innocuous operation of a tooth extraction in the autumn of 1846. News of the true identity of Letheon had by this time reached England, and on 19 December 1846 the anaesthetic was used in London also for a tooth extraction. Two days later, however, on 21 December, the medium was put to a far more substantial test. Robert Liston, the most sensational surgeon of his age, used ether in a major operation. To call Liston *sensational* is not to be sensational. A surgeon in the first half of the nineteenth century had above all to be adept at speed, because before the age of anaesthetics his patient, even if previously rendered roaring drunk on rum, could not endure the pain of a live amputation for more than a minimum period of time. A surgeon had therefore to have the skill of a conjuror. The quickness of his hand had at least to deceive the patient. His confrères used to say that when Liston amputated 'the gleam of the knife was followed so instantaneously by the sound of sawing as to make the two actions appear almost simultaneous' – and it is to be hoped that his patients appreciated this speed since they saw the knife, felt the cut and heard the sawing. Liston put a patient under ether on that December day of 1846 while he amputated a thigh. That so eminent a surgeon should commit himself to this then untried anaesthetic was historically mind-changing, and within a very short time the administration of ether became general in hospitals in Europe and America. Liston himself did not survive to comment on the sequel to his pioneering decision, for he died in the following year. In his hospital – University College Hospital, London, where he was Professor of Clinical Surgery – there was at that time a first-year student whose name has sometimes been confused with Liston's. This was Joseph Lister, afterwards Lord Lister and the first medical man to be raised to the peerage besides being a founder member of King Edward VII's creation of the Order of Merit. Joseph Lister was a surgeon who specialised in his early research on muscle cells, inflammation, gangrene and blood coagulation. Later he became deeply concerned at the number of deaths due to wound infection, and he recognised that the immediate danger to be conquered in the medical conditions of his day was the threat of sepsis or blood poisoning following surgery. It was his concentration on destroying the bacteria already existing in wounds and on applying dressings impregnated with a bactericide – in the first instance, carbolic acid – that prompted the other great surgical advance of a century ago. Lister first drew attention to his mighty preoccupation by two historic papers published in the *Lancet* in 1867. He literally cleaned up the hospitals of this country by drastic measures against infection, introduced among other innovations the carbolised catgut suture, and by his insistence on sterile conditions in the operating theatre virtually made internal surgical operations possible. Liston as the pioneer of anaesthetics, and Lister as the messiah of antiseptics, are therefore the heroes of British and world surgery, not just of a century ago but for all time.

Ether and nitrous oxide as anaesthetics were followed by chloroform, which had been discovered in 1831 and was first used a year after Liston initiated the administration of ether, on 15 November 1847 when Professor (later Sir) James Young Simpson, who held the chair of midwifery at Edinburgh, used it in the delivery of a baby, on the expert advice of a Liverpool surgeon named Waldie. Chloroform rapidly supplanted ether in hospital use in Europe, since it was believed to be faster, more controllable, and safer. This was not entirely true, especially with regard to the rather crude conditions under which it was first administered, and a death on the theatre table from the administration of chloroform occurred within two months of its first use. Until the effects of anaesthetics were more carefully studied, and its somewhat slap-happy use more stringently controlled, there were a number of early casualties from the administration of this pain-killing wonder in whatever form it was presented. But Victorian women were in no doubt about the blessing that chloroform had brought them to see them through childbirth. James Young Simpson's first patient, the wife of an Edinburgh doctor, had been so emphatic about the bliss it had brought her that she christened the daughter he had delivered Anaesthesia. A far more influential cachet was given to the use of the drug some five years later. At the age of 33, after twelve years of marriage, Queen Victoria was expecting her eighth child. Victoria detested not only the pain but the mechanics of childbirth. She thought it reduced women to the status of cows. She therefore requested her surgeon, Sir James Clark, to consider the administration 'of chloroform. Clark wrote to Simpson in Edinburgh and Simpson sent down his anaesthetist, Dr John Snow. Public opinion was at that time engaged with the usual battle between the modernists and the fundamentalists that has always attended any great scientific innovation. The fundamentalists said it was the will of God that childbirth should be excruciating, and quoted the words of the Lord to Eve in Eden: 'In sorrow thou shalt bring forth children'. The modernists retorted that God had at least approved anaesthetics for men since when Eve was created from Adam's body in that same garden of Eden 'The Lord caused a deep sleep to fall on Adam'. Whether or not it was a protest against male chauvinism, Queen Victoria certainly ordered that a deep sleep should fall on her. Dr Snow obeyed her command and rolled a handkerchief into a funnel down which he poured a half-teaspoonful of chloroform towards the Queen's mouth and nose. Sir James Clark afterwards told Simpson that it had not been enough to render the Monarch unconscious: 'It was not at any time given so strongly as to render the Queen insensible, and an ounce of chloroform was scarcely consumed during the whole time. Her Majesty was greatly pleased with the effect, and she certainly never has had a better recovery'.

Queen Victoria was far less clinically reserved. She wrote in her diary: 'Dr Snow gave that blessed Chloroform & the effect was soothing, quieting & delightful beyond measure'. This royal endorsement of 7 April 1853, naturally not published at the time, though the fact that she had opted for chloroform was widely known, was 'perhaps the most influential single act of the Queen's career, unconnected as it was with politics or affairs of state but bearing immediately on the reactions of every woman in the country. Through no fault of the doctors concerned the baby who was born, Prince Leopold, suffered from the bleeding disease – the only positive haemophiliac in her family of nine children, though three of Victoria's daughters, while not suffering it, transmitted it by their marriages through the royal families of Russia, Prussia and Spain. Leopold, though always delicate, lived into maturity and married, but died when he was 31. His daughter, Princess Alice, afterwards Countess of Athlone, who was a putative carrier and had no children, was in St Paul's Cathedral and on the balcony of Buckingham Palace during the Jubilee celebrations of Queen Elizabeth II in 1977, one hundred and twenty four years after the birth of her father in the 'delightful circumstances' induced by 'that blessed Chloroform'.

SEVEN
OFFENSIVE WEAPONS

THE MID-NINETEENTH CENTURY was a period of fast and drastic change in naval architecture, naval armament and naval armour. It marked the end of three romantic centuries of sail in the service of the Sovereign, culminating in the wooden walls of the line-of-battle ships which, after Trafalgar, had worn the White Ensign with increasing honour in every ocean of the world. It was the end of an age of glamour whose charisma has never been revived. C. S. Forester never chose to write novels about turret ships on the West Indies station, and Captain Marryat declined to place Mr Midshipman Easy and his other heroes in hybrid ironclads – although Marryat, serving in the Burma War in 1824, suggested and had his proposal approved that HMS *Diana* should be used as the first steamship to be employed on active service in the Royal Navy. It was the beginning of the Crimean War in 1854 which marked the beginnings of the new ungainly ironclad Navy, and abolished the word *frigate* as a symbol of picturesque good looks for a full century, after which the lines as well as the operations of the new frigates have taken on a new grace. The French Emperor Napoleon III began the employment of floating batteries plated with iron with the operations of the new war, and this innovation immediately brought into prominence the matter of protecting warships with some kind of defensive armour, since artillery was advancing faster than armour, and the new guns adopted by the navies could fire shot with a potentiality to pierce with the greatest facility the hulls of any wooden ship afloat. And so the race in naval armour and armament began. Although we were, in the Crimean War, the allies of the French, this was an entirely novel situation which took a long time to become established in national thinking. The French were our traditional enemies, whom we had fought consistently for well over a century, and any improvement in their navy had to be matched in ours. The French built *La Gloire*, a timber-framed ship covered with an armour of iron plates $4\frac{1}{2}$ inches thick. The British promptly laid down the *Warrior*, with the lines of an old wooden frigate but built on an iron frame with armour plating of the same thickness as *La Gloire*'s additionally backed by eighteen inches of solid teak all round and an inner skin of iron. This iron cladding over massive timber was adopted for succeeding British warships and was sufficient to withstand the 68-pound shot that was momentarily the maximum projectile being fired. But the power of naval artillery increased speedily. One of the results was that the guns became more concentrated. In the *Warrior* there were still guns by the score ranged all along the sides of the vessel and firing through ports to give what was really no more than the old Nelsonian broadside. The action of the guns was the same as on the *Victory*, with the guns recoiling after fire and being shoved back again, although they no longer ran on wooden wheels, but used iron wheels running on short rails. In later naval ship design the guns, six times the weight and firing far more destructive shot than the old 68-pounders, were grouped in separate batteries and reduced in number. But for a few more years warships in the main could still only fire broadsides for any real effect in battle. Apart from the old conventional stern-chaser and a forward gun which was little more than a saluting weapon, the men-of-war had to steam towards the enemy and then veer round to fire a broadside if they were to be offensively operative. One of the last great ships obeying this old design was the *Hercules*. She was roughly twice the tonnage of the old *Victory* – 5226 tons, with a length of 325 feet and a beam of 59 feet. She was a very powerful craft, fitted with engines which would work up to a declared 8529 horse power. Her bulk weight, as compared with her displacement tonnage was enormous: her hull was 4022 tons with an additional 1690 tons of armour and backing; fully loaded with fuel her engines, boilers and coals weighed 1826 tons; her equipment and armament weighed a massive 8676 tons. Carrying all this impedimenta she could still steam at 17 knots and was remarkably handy, with a turning circle of 560 yards diameter which could be accomplished in four minutes. She was constructed with the double hull which the *Great Eastern* had demonstrated as a highly desirable property. Her defensive armour reached a maximum of nine inches of plating on the waterline, backed by solid teak of from ten to twelve inches depth which swelled to nearly four feet on the vulnerable waterline, with an additional iron plating on the inner skin of two and a quarter inches. The deck also was covered by iron plates to withstand shot tearing it up. She carried as her central battery eight 18-ton rifled guns firing 400-pound shot, and she had 12-ton guns in her bow and stern. The guns of the broadside still fired through ports, but with indented ports and turntable carriages the guns could fire at an acute angle of fifteen degrees from the keel. Her armour had been tested to take a 600-pound shot from 700 yards without being penetrated. As an alternative design, a faster ship had been built, the *Inconstant*, as the fore-runner of a class which was ironclad but not strictly armoured, carrying ten rifled nine-inch (twelve-ton) guns and six seven-inch (six-ton) guns, and her 6500 horse-power engines could reach a speed of $18\frac{1}{2}$ knots with her lighter load.

In 1861 Captain Coles of the Royal Navy proposed a new design of ship which was a logical development of the principle of concentrating naval guns into a battery. He designed and perfected a low circular turret, built on the deck and heavily armoured, carrying one or two heavy guns which could revolve in full circle. This design was accepted and the Admiralty commissioned two ships to be built on these principles, the *Captain* and the *Monarch*. They were three-masters, capable of carrying a full spread of sail as an auxiliary to the steam engines driving twin screws of 17 feet diameter. Because there were not only masts but deck-housing on the main deck, the revolving turrets could not in fact train their guns dead fore and aft, but could fire up to an angle of six degrees to the keel. The turrets were 27 feet in their exterior diameter and 22 feet 6 inches internally, having walls over two feet thick of which the iron armour plate was one foot thick. They each carried two 25-ton guns which fired 600-pound shot, and the turrets could be revolved manually or by steam power. The ships had two skins and the armour plating on the outside hull was eight inches on twelve inches of teak and extending five feet below the waterline. The armour plating on the deck was an inch and a half thick. That the vessel was carrying a huge weight was clear from the sea trials of the *Captain*, when it was seen that the freeboard was eighteen inches shallower than designed, being six and a half feet instead of eight feet. Nevertheless, the *Captain* was sent out with the Fleet on an autumn cruise. Off Cape

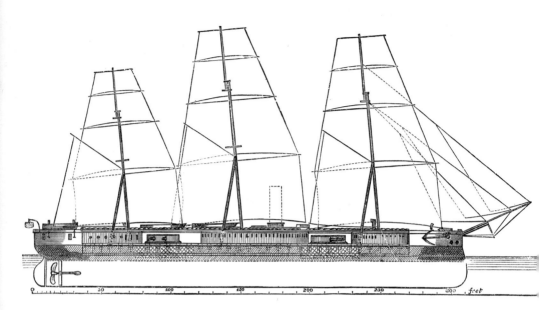

HMS *Captain.*

Finisterre, Brittany, on the night of 6–7 September 1870 in squally weather with a heavy sea running, the *Captain* turned turtle and took her crew of five hundred to the bottom, the designer Captain Coles included, except for sixteen petty officers and men, and three boys, who managed to reach the shore. One of the survivors, Gunner James May, told the subsequent Court of Enquiry that he had been awoken by an unexplained noise shortly after midnight and he recognised from long experience at sea that the ship was responding uneasily. He took a light and went to check the guns in the after turret. While he was inside the turret he felt the ship steadily heel over. A heavy sea struck from the weather side and rushed into the turret. He struggled out of the hole in the side of the turret which was the gun embrasure, squeezing himself between the gun barrel and the aperture in the armour plating, and immediately found himself in the sea. He swam to the steam-pinnace, which was floating bottom upwards, where he was joined by his commanding officer, Captain Burgoyne, and one or two others. They saw the *Captain* turn completely upside down and sink stern first within a few minutes of its heeling over. A launch with sixteen members of the deck watch drifted near the upturned pinnace, and May and three others jumped into it. One of the watch who was already in the launch had actually walked off the inverted bottom of the ship into the boat. The boat crew saw that their captain had not succeeded in jumping from the pinnace, and they turned back to search for him but could not find him in the dark and stormy water. One man was washed out of their own launch in the search. The survivors set to the oars and after twelve hours' hard rowing they came ashore at Cape Finisterre.

The *Captain* had capsized because of her inherent instability after a series of oscillations which, by bad luck, were more severe than normal expectation could anticipate because they exactly coincided in frequency with the gusts of the squally weather, and she was in fact carried over by the pressure of wind on her sails and the additional push of a hurricane squall on the underside of the vessel as she lay heeled over. Her successor in naval design, already on the stocks, was built to avoid every one of these perils except for the fact that she had a freeboard of only three feet at the maximum. She was launched the following year. This was the Monitor class *Glatton*, designed by Sir Edward Reed, Constructor to the Navy, a powerful warship which was considered a century ago to be an impregnable floating fortress. She carried no sail at all, her single mast being used only for signalling and hauling up boats. She had one turret, placed comparatively high compared with the *Captain* and entirely unimpeded for firing over the bow. The turret armament was the same as with the *Captain*, but it was even more heavily armoured, having iron plating 14 inches thick and a protective breastwork rising six feet above the deck. She was so designed that her three-feet free-board could be reduced to two feet when in action by pumping in an additional tonnage of water into the lowest compartment, and in this trim she presented a very shallow target indeed. With her enormous weight of armour plating – up to twelve inches of iron on twenty inches of teak on the main hull – she had a low speed of some 9½ knots and was intended for a coast defence rather than ocean-going rôle, which at least preserved her from exposure to the storms of Cape Finisterre. Two additionally powerful turret ships were constructed after the successful trials of the *Glatton*. These were the sisterships *Devastation* and *Thunderer*, having turrets fore and aft instead of the *Glatton*'s single turret, and carrying nearly four times as much coal so that they had an optimum cruising distance of 3000 miles at twelve knots. The turrets were armoured with five layers of iron and teak alternately, with altogether seventeen inches of armour plate and fifteen inches of teak. Their armament had now been stepped up to 35-ton guns taking a charge of 120 pounds of powder to discharge shot weighing 700 pounds with an estimated destructive power of 8404 foot-tons at a range of 1000 yards. These guns had been built at the Royal Gun Factory to the design of its director, named Fraser, who had improved on the pattern of rifled cannon designed by Sir William Armstrong after Armstrong resigned his post as Chief Engineer of Rifled Ordnance at Woolwich in 1863. The Fraser gun used cheaper iron than the Armstrong gun and was made in only four parts instead of ten. These parts were: 1., the rifled inner steel barrel toughened to achieve maximum hardness and tenacity; 2., the B tube, enclosing the mouth end of the barrel and continuing back for about half its length, made of two double coils of iron bars, welded, hammered and bored; 3., the breech-coil or jacket, a much thicker mass enclosing the breech and made of triple coils of iron; and, 4., the cascabel screw, the solid iron piece screwed into the rear of the gun which had to resist the force tending to blow out the gunner's end of the barrel. A 35-ton Fraser gun was about sixteen feet long, 4 feet 8 inches in diameter at the breech and one foot nine inches at the muzzle, with a

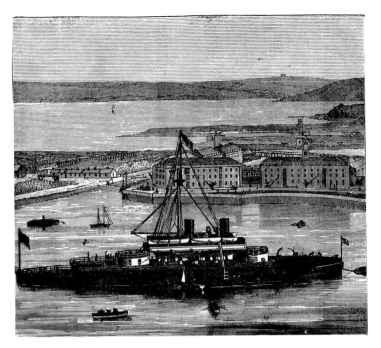

HMS *Devastation* in Queenstown Harbour.

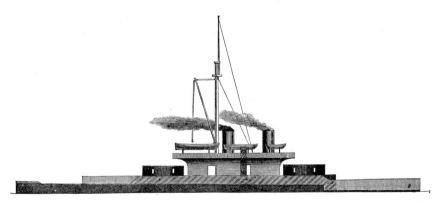

HMS *Thunderer*.

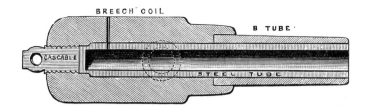

Section of a 9 inch Fraser gun.

The 35 ton Fraser gun.

bore of one foot. Its 700-pound shot fired by 120 pounds of powder would penetrate a twelve-inch iron plate at 2000 yards and a fourteen-inch plate at shorter range. It cost, a century ago, £2500 to produce as against £3500 for an Armstrong gun of similar weight and £6000 for a Whitworth gun. Sir Joseph Whitworth's artillery was finer material, always made of steel, exceedingly accurate and with what was then an enormous range. A Whitworth breech-loader then threw a 250-pound shot fired by fifty pounds of powder a distance of nearly six miles.

Fraser's 35-ton gun, the pride of Woolwich Arsenal a century ago, was about to be dwarfed by a new gun, then approved, designed to weigh 81 tons with a length of bore of 24 feet and a diameter of bore of fourteen inches – or sixteen inches if that could be managed – and firing shot of 1000 pounds and 1200 pounds. Krupps, in Germany, were already producing 110-ton siege guns. The ordnance department at Woolwich was really rather prouder of its seven-pounder rifled steel gun – which even on its wheeled gun-carriage was like a toy not coming up to a man's thigh – an accurate weapon weighing only 148 pounds in all which used half a pound of gunpowder to fire its seven-pound shell with great precision over a thousand yards. In the colonial wars of the period it had been found admirable for mountain warfare and for rough country where heavier artillery would be difficult to transport. The British Army was still sounding the praises of the performance of this gun in Abyssinia, where Napier had led an expedition in 1868 after its King had imprisoned British and European ambassadors and missionaries: 'In the battle which preceded the fall of Magdala and the death of King Theodore, the shells thrown by these little guns at a distance of several hundred yards cut up and threw into confusion the great bodies of men which the Abyssinian King had collected.'

In the Abyssinian campaign the British Army was making its first practical assessment of breech-loading rifles, though the equipment it had been issued with was markedly second-rate. A decade before, in the Indian Mutiny, the rifles had been muzzle-loaders; the bullet and powder were wrapped together in a paper cylinder; before firing, the end of the cylinder was bitten off, the gunpowder poured down the muzzle, and the bullet and cartridge-paper rammed down on top; and the report that the cartridge-paper which had to be bitten had been previously smeared with the fat both of the cow and the pig consequently proved highly successful propaganda to make dissidents out of both

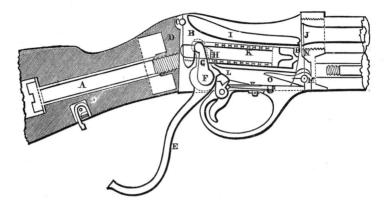

Section of a Martini-Henry lock.

The Martini-Henry rifle: above, ready for loading; below, ready for firing.

Hindu and Moslem sepoy soldiers. The breech-loader was clearly a far more efficient arm, but it never became a practical possibility in battle until the invention of the percussion cap for firing the charge. When this happened, a British Government committee met in 1864 with the task of determining what gun the infantry should be issued with. They strongly recommended the breech-loader but could not find a suitable model. They therefore urged that the old muzzle-loading Enfield rifle then in service should be converted for a pound a weapon by fitting a Snider breech, and that in the meantime British gunsmiths should be rounded up in a competition to design the best breech-loading rifle which would accord with the specifications laid down. The competition was held in 1866. There were 104 entrants. The committee did not award a first prize, and they gave the second prize to an inventor called Henry who had concentrated on a patent rifling system and a bullet which would best accommodate itself to the heptagonal (seven-sided) bore. The committee then set about the arduous task of deciding on the best combination of barrel, bore, rifling, cartridge and – by a seemingly very casual order of preference – system of breech-loading. But that part of the competition had apparently already been decided in favour of the mechanism proposed by Frederic Martini, a Hungarian-born engineer who had established a machine works at Frauenfeld in Switzerland. Martini had, however, only achieved seventh place in the competition. It was unimportant, for the subsequent royalties were tremendous. The decision went to the construction of a Martini-Henry rifle, using Martini's breech and Henry's rifling. The poor bloody infantry in Abyssinia having been issued with the cheapjack Snider-Enfield conversion, the new service weapon was issued in 1871 when there was no prospect of a reasonably testing war for some time. The Martini-Henry rifle had a steel barrel 33.22 inches long and 0.451 inches in bore. There were seven grooves in the rifling with a twist once in 22 inches, so that the bullet was turned through one and a half revolutions before it emerged from the muzzle. The charge consisted of 85 grains of powder (just under one fifth of an ounce). The bullet weighed 480 grains (1.1 ounces). The cartridge was bottle-shaped, which allowed it to be shorter and stronger. A wad of bees-wax was placed between the bullet and the powder, so that the barrel was lubricated at every discharge. The rifle took a sword-bayonet weighing a pound and a half and two feet one and a half inches in length, a broad blade with a double row of teeth on the blunt edge of the sword which, though it would undoubtedly inflict a deal of painful damage on an unlucky recipient, was justified by its theoretical purpose 'useful for cutting and sawing brushwood, small trees, etc., in addition to its primary use as a bayonet.' The Martini-Henry was sighted to 1400 yards and, having been tested for accuracy at 1200 yards, recorded over twenty shots a mean absolute deflection of the hits from the centre of the target of 2.28 feet. It was then held highly important that it had a very low trajectory, rising to about eight feet from the ground over 500 yards, which, it was estimated, would hit any cavalry trooper's head within that distance. The Snider-Enfield had a trajectory of twelve feet at that range. The bullet of the Martini-Henry would pass through from thirteen to seventeen half-inch elm planks placed one inch apart when fired from twenty yards, which was double the penetration power of the Snider-Enfield. On the score of rapidity of fire its best performance was twenty rounds in 53 seconds.

That was an execution that could then be excelled only by the machine guns, or *mitrailleurs*, of the 1870s. (The French word, which comes from a contrived verb meaning to scatter small missiles, was later feminised to *mitrailleuse*.) The French mitrailleur was greatly huffed and puffed by the French Army before the Franco-Prussian War of 1870, just as the Maginot Line was lauded in 1939; but as the German General Staff had taken both considerations into account, and circumvented them by superior strategy, it is likely that a true appreciation of either defence is difficult to assess because of the counter-productivity of the items as failed propaganda. *Before* the onset of the 1870 war, but in the same year, a British military committee assessed the mitrailleur against the Gatling, and although the Gatling jammed far too often – as it always did in action – the professional view favoured it against the French weapon.

The Gatling Battery Gun was invented by the American Richard Jordan Gatling in 1861, and over the next four years during the American Civil War he had plenty of opportunity to improve it. It was shaped like a small field gun, with a carriage, but what should have been the barrel was in fact ten rifled barrels fixed in a circle. The machine was cranked like a mincing machine, which was what it set out to be, and cartridges dropped from a feeder into the grooves as the cylinder was hand-rotated, and were locked, fired and ejected. The gun came in three sizes, firing in the largest model half-pound bullets one inch in diameter,

The Gatling Battery Gun.

The Montigny Mitrailleur.

and in the smallest model ordinary .45 bullets. The small Gatling was
advertised as capable of firing 400 bullets in a minute, after which (if it
had not jammed) it had to be re-loaded, and it was claimed to be
effective at a distance of a mile and a quarter. In a military test at 800
yards range against targets representing columns of infantry and
cavalry, when the Gatling was matched against the Montigny mitrailleur, a twelve-pounder breech-loader and a nine-pounder muzzle-loaded
rifled gun, the Gatling came second to the breech-loader in the number
of estimated casualties it caused. It beat the muzzle-loader apparently
only for the reason that this gun, out of seven rounds, fired two pre-
maturely and had one ineffective 'burst over'. But the shrapnel scattered
by the muzzle-loader was most effective when it struck. Shrapnel,
which had been used by the British Army since 1803, had been so
effectively improved by the 1870s that an exercise on Dartmoor pur-
ported to show that a single field battery, advantageously placed and
firing the improved shrapnel shell, could kill or disable 20,000 men in an
hour.

EIGHT
NEW TECHNIQUES

ONE OF THE MOST significant areas in which Victorian wonders were historically important was in the sphere of *record*. It was for this reason that the Victorian invention of photography was chiefly valued, by the Victorians – as a means of record. Whether it was an art or not could be developed, discussed, and exploited later. The immediate advantage, as it was then seen, was that it added to their ability to render an accurate and reliable account of what had passed – even what had passed only half an hour ago. (The dictum that 'the camera cannot lie' had not then been coined, but it was generally enough believed, and indeed it is a good enough generalisation a century and a half later.) Allowing for a certain overgrown grandeur of literary style, there was a sensible basis in the attitude of the Victorian who declared of photography: 'It exercises a beneficial influence over the social sentiments, the arts, the sciences of the whole world – an influence not the less real because it is wide spread and unobtrusive. It cherishes domestic and friendly feelings by its ever-present transcripts of familiar faces, keeping fresh the memory of the distant and the dead. It keeps alive our admiration of the great and the good by presenting us with the lineaments of the heroes, the saints and the sages of all lands. It gratifies, by faithful portrayals of scenes of grandeur, and of beauty, the eyes of him who has neither wealth or leisure for travel. It has improved pictorial art by sending the painter to the truths of nature. It has reproduced his works with marvellous fidelity. It has set before the multitude the finest works of the sculptor. It is lending valuable aid to almost every science. The astronomer now derives his mathematical data from the photograph. By its aid the architect superintends the erection of distant buildings, the engineer watches over the progress of his designs in distant lands, the medical man amasses records of morbid anatomy, the geologist studies the anatomy of the earth, the ethnologist obtains faithful transcripts of the features of every race. No other of our nineteenth century inventions is at once so beautiful, so precious, so popular, so valuable an aid to knowledge.'

It was indeed a wholly nineteenth century progression. In 1802 Josiah Wedgwood's son Thomas published a report of the experimental work he had carried out with Humphry Davy in recording profiles and copying paintings on glass by the action of light on silver nitrate. The images they had obtained could not be fixed because they as yet knew no means of removing the emulsion of silver salts from the unaffected parts of the white paper or white leather with which they had been experimenting. In 1814 the Frenchman Joseph Niepce was able to obtain a permanent picture by what he then termed heliography. He smeared a highly polished metal plate with a film of a bituminous subtance which he called 'bitumen of Judaea' and exposed this plate within a camera obscura for several hours. The action of the light had a chemical effect on the emulsion. Previously it had been soluble in oil of lavender. After exposure to the light it was insoluble. When he dipped the plate in oil of lavender after his heliography, the solvent worked only on those portions of the plate where there had been deep shadows. These parts were dissolved away, but where the light had fallen strongly the bitumen was undissolved. The brightly polished parts of the plate which had been uncovered appeared dark when they were made to reflect dark objects, while the bitumen remaining on the plate appeared light by comparison. Louis Daguerre was impressed by his work, and eventually got in touch with Niepce. Daguerre had started life as an inland revenue officer, but understandably revolted against his duties and became an artist. By specialisation he established a pictorial exhibition called the diorama, and he was successful enough to open a similar exhibition in London. His strong ambition was to produce permanent pictures by means of sunlight and to this end he joined with Niepce. Niepce subsequently died, but Daguerre persisted and eventually invented a process by which he could reproduce pictures showing shadows, highlights and half-tints faithfully enough after exposure in a camera for only twenty minutes. He used a plate of burnished copper, coated with pure silver and highly polished again, then exposed the prepared plate to the fumes of iodine vapour until a uniform yellow film had settled uniformly on the surface. He exposed this plate and then developed it by allowing mercury vapour to act on it, and as a result the mercury became attached to the various areas of the plate in proportion as they had been acted on by the light. Daguerre then invented a means of fixing the picture and published the results of his discoveries. He continued to improve the process, notably by the use of bromine as well as iodine, increasing the sensitivity of the plate until an exposure of only two minutes was necessary. His daguerrotypes were accepted as attractive positive records by 1841.

But six months before Daguerre's original publication in 1839 the Englishman William Henry Fox Talbot – a polymath typical of the Victorian age who worked in the fields of mathematics, optics, the chemistry of colour, botany and philology – published his entirely independent findings of a process for preparing sensitive paper for copying prints by coating the paper first with silver chloride and then passing light through the paper of the print so that those parts of the sensitive paper protected by the opaque black lines of the print were not acted on by the light. In this way he obtained a negative print, and by repeating the process with the negative and another sheet of sensitive paper he obtained a positive. This image was fixed by a solution of silver chloride and potassium bromide, but very soon Fox Talbot used sodium hyposulphite to dissolve out the unwanted silver, and the main process of photography as it was later to develop was founded. A glass plate coated with albumen was later substituted for the original paper which had been used for the negative, and later collodion was used as the vehicle for the sensitive salts. This was the extremely effective, though messy, wet-plate process. By 1871 Dr R. L. Maddox had introduced a gelatine emulsion to hold the silver bromide salts, which produced the dry plate and, by abolishing the previous necessity for a portable dark room, set photography well within the grasp of the not too technical amateur. This was in fact as far as the craft had gone a century ago, for Eastman did not introduce celluloid roll films until 1884. But throughout the nineteenth century the physicists were aware of the phenomena that indicated the possibility of colour photography, but did not have the knowledge, experience and luck to be able to duplicate the process at their own time and by their own choice.

One of the men who tried to crack the problem of colour photography was Sir John Herschel, the astronomer son of the astronomer Sir William Herschel, and the man who, exemplifying the grand way in which the Victorians ignored any hedges set up by jealous specialists to cut up the broad highway of knowledge into narrow lanes of restricted disciplines, was the pioneer who introduced 'hypo' for fixing in photography and also was able to knock off a spell of five years as Master of the Mint. Herschel once observed that a principal factor – and he declared that it was even a principal cause – of the rapid development of the physical sciences in his age was the improvement in scientific apparatus and particularly in instruments for making measurements or exact observations. To achieve the reliably accurate and elaborate instruments which were required for the precise determinations and observations of the active scientists of the time demanded a previous precision and accuracy in the toolmakers as well as an exact knowledge on the part of the scientists of what they were commissioning the toolmakers to do. Some very telling examples of what was specified, and what was produced, may be mentioned. A recording anemometer made by Apps – a famous instrument-constructor with a shop in the Strand in London – registered the force and direction of the wind without supervision and recorded it continuously at all times of the day. Professor Hough of Dudley Observatory designed and commissioned a metereograph which performed the functions of both a barometer and a thermometer and recorded the readings of both instruments with a single piece of mechanism and on the same sheet of paper. It was Hough who invented the continuous-line recorder for both temperature and pressure (the latter to a thousandth of an inch) by the movement of an inked needle on an endless drum of paper. An invention which had several simultaneous originators or adaptors was the electrochronograph for measuring small intervals of time. It was used by Professor Bashforth to measure the speed of artillery missiles by placing screens at measured intervals in the path of the projectile. In medicine the instrument makers constructed a sphygmograph for recording variations in the pulse, the circulatory system and the heart. They also produced the spirograph which gave a detailed record of the condition of the lungs and the respiratory system. And for submarine and meteorological observations the old-established firm of Negretti and Zambra (which provided virtually a public weather-recording and forecasting office before the national Meteorological

Office realised the value of the publicity) constructed a deep-sea thermometer capable of operating at 3000 fathoms – that is, at a pressure of three tons to the square inch of thermometer-glass – or, among many other productions in its dossier, an atmospheric recording thermometer and wet- and dry-bulb hygrometer which took observations for observatories at regular intervals as long as the automatic machinery could be persuaded to run.

Digging, sorting, and washing diamonds in the diamond fields of
South Africa.

NINE
NEW MATERIALS

RUBBER WAS NEVER commercially applied, or even used to erase a pencil mark, until it began to be commercially imported in 1820. It had been known and brought home as a souvenir or traveller's curiosity before then. It had existed in Peru, its natural habitat, for time beyond record. (It was because of the Peruvian Indians who collected it that it was at first called Indian-rubber, not India-rubber as is now generally thought – and the *rubber* name was merely a reference to the fact that it could rub out pencil marks and that was its first and solitary use.) It came from the milky juice of tropical plants grown mainly in the forests of the basin of the river Amazon. Manufacturing interest was aroused in its potentiality and in the year of its first importation, 1820, a number of patents were taken out for the use of crude rubber for braces, garters, elastic-sided boots and the wrists of gloves, to be used instead of laces. A treatment was then devised for working up crude rubber by warmth and pressure in order that it could be shaped into boot-soles. Charles Macintosh, a Glasgow chemist, found a way of dissolving rubber so that clothing could be varnished with the solution, and invented the waterproof garments which still bear his name. By 1840 Charles Goodyear, a failed American ironmaster, developed after suffering years of poverty a method of vulcanising rubber to overcome its stickiness in warm temperatures and its rigidity in cold, and started selling waterproof boots, which made him a satisfactory fortune before the great demand for automobile tyres set in. A century ago, when there were no motor cars, the principal uses of rubber were for carriage tyres, carriage springs, the rollers of mangles, a variety of uses for saving life at sea such as in portable boats, pontoons, life-buoys and deep-sea diving outfits – and

[131]

domestically for a hundred varieties of cushion from air-beds to billiard tables. Hardened with sulphur to produce what was called vulcanite, or ebonite, it was manufactured, among many other uses, into combs and buttons and every sort of insulating support in electrical machines and fittings. The success of rubber prompted the import into Europe in 1822 of gutta-percha, a chemically similar substance solidified from the juice of a tree common in Borneo and Malacca, but unlike rubber in appearance, being generally imported as hard red-brown cakes which emit a cheesy smell when cut. Gutta-percha was and is a very tough substance but without the elasticity of rubber. It had a wax-like character in that it became softened by gentle heat and in that state would take and retain any impressions with great sharpness and fidelity. Before the invention of the telephone gutta-percha tubing was installed in many noble mansions and large commercial buildings as very efficient speaking tubes. Because of its quality as a non-conductor it was mainly used as an insulating cover for telegraph wires and particularly submarine cables.

Petroleum, which literally means rock-oil, had been known as a casually occurring natural phenomenon since the thirteenth century in Burma, from which time hand-dug wells were made for mineral oil around Rangoon. It was also known around the Caspian Sea. Odd accidental findings of the oil in America set geologists and commercial speculators scheming. It was as late as August 1859 that the first mechanically-bored well in the world was drilled by Edwin Drake at Oil Creek, Pennsylvania, and Drake struck oil at a supply rate of 1000 gallons a day. That started the oil boom and the oil-crazy speculation all over North America, including Canada where there was much early success. A century ago the production of petroleum was confined to the North American continent, from where it was exported all over the world as the cheapest available illuminating and lubricating oil. Its use as automobile fuel was still undreamed of.

Paraffin, which in its pure state is a solid at normal temperatures, is a constituent of petroleum, but was discovered in England in close connection with coal. In 1847 Dr Lyon Playfair noticed a thick mineral oil issuing from crevices of coal in a Derbyshire mine. This substance could be treated to yield a distillation of a pale yellow oil which on cooling deposited solid paraffin. The coal mine where it was found was immediately converted to the extraction of this paraffin. When that area was exhausted a fresh source was found in a bituminous coalfield at Boghead near Bathgate in Linlithgow. Pure paraffin was used at a rate of thousands of tons annually for making candles, and after treatment as paraffin-wax was used to line food-containers and beer-barrels. What was inaccurately but popularly called paraffin in Great Britain was kerosine oil for heating and lighting (and now for jet aircraft fuel) which is a hydrocarbon distilled from petroleum.

Among new metals which were produced in a pure form in the nineteenth century, potassium was separated in 1807 by Sir Humphry Davy who achieved the electrical fusion of caustic potash, isolated potassium, and almost immediately afterwards obtained sodium by the same method. Aluminium was first isolated in 1827 by Œrsted, who decomposed aluminium chloride with potassium, but this laboratory success was not enlarged into a successful commercial process until 1854 when the firm of Bell, of Newcastle, began the practical manufacture of aluminium according to a process initiated by De Ville. A century ago its notable lightness had encouraged its use for ornamental work, for casting, and for the parts of implements where lightness and rigidity were necessary such as the tubes of telescopes, the beams of balances, or the frames of opera glasses, but its later extensive use in transport had not then been foreseen. The metal magnesium was first prepared in 1830 by the French chemist Bussy using a process similar to that by which De Ville later obtained aluminium. Its commercial production took about as long to develop as that of aluminium. Its chief use was for burning as magnesium wire for dazzling artificial light, as used in flash photography and in firework displays.

It is an unsuspected surprise today to realise that the minerals which burst into most sensational supply in the third quarter of the nineteenth century were gold and diamonds. The first sighting of gold in California occurred in September 1847, when the proprietor of a saw-mill on the Sacramento River, a man called Marshall, saw some glistening grains among the sand in his mill-race. By 1849 the existence of deposits had been confirmed, and the Gold Rush was on. The next stampede was to the Klondike district of Yukon, Alaska. The worldwide fever for gold-prospecting led to the Australians taking a closer look at their own soil. The geologist Sir Roderick Murchison had pointed out long previously that the rock formation in parts of the continent implied a probability that gold existed in Australia. He had not seen it, because he was not there, but at least he got a goldfield in Western Australia named after him when the discovery was finally made. Considering the manner in which gold occurs, it is strange that the early immigrants who mainly raised sheep and cattle did not notice the glittering particles which were on occasion apparent in the shallow beds of the water-courses where their grazing herds drank. After the details had been absorbed of the gold in the sands of the California mill-race the Australians kept a livelier eye open for these traces, and by April 1851 a Mr Hargeaves of Bathurst had found it. Four months later what was to prove the beginning of an even richer field was found at Ballarat, Victoria. The discovery increased Victoria's population ninefold in sixteen years, and swelled the area of land under cultivation by an even greater proportion. In those first few years over 36 million ounces of gold had been extracted from the Victoria fields with a value of over £147 million. The largest nugget picked up at Ballarat weighed 183 pounds.

Diamonds had only one source during most of the history of the adoring appreciation of the gem: they came from the mines of Golconda in Hindustan and nowhere else. But in the eighteenth century they were discovered in Brazil and a regular supply from this source began. This was the situation until 1867, when some children playing near the banks of the Orange River in South Africa found what they thought was a pretty pebble. A neighbour saw it in their hands, and gave their mother a trifle for it and took it away. It passed through several hands, and finally was bought by the Governor of the colony for £500. Shortly afterwards, other diamonds were discovered in the same area, and in even greater frequency on the banks of the Vaal River. A Diamond Rush even more feverish than the Californian Gold Rush was now begun, and a century ago, when all the Victorian wonders were the subjects of assessment and speculation, the future of the new diamond-mining was the least certain, the most speculative – as it has continued to be for a further uncertain and speculative century.

A NOTE ON THE TYPEFACE

This book was composed on the Monotype in Old Style Series 2, a type that has its origin in the revival of Caslon's old face by William Pickering and Charles Whittingham of the Chiswick Press in the 1840s. The success of this revival led the Edinburgh type foundry of Miller & Richard to cut this present, modernised version which had become by 1900 the standard alternative to the modern face of the nineteenth-century printing office. Old Style is thinner and more angular than old face and may be considered as a 'transitional' face between the earlier form and the modern face. The serif is short and stubby, and the contrast between thick and thins is not very stressed. The complete fount shows a pleasing uniformity of design devoid of letterform eccentricities of any kind. Series 2 was cut by the Monotype Corporation in 1901 and was the second text face to be made available for composition on Monotype machines.